A CURATE
FOR ALL SEASONS

D1463930

Fred Secombe

A CURATE
FOR ALL SEASONS

—

Illustrated by Maxine Rogers

Fount

An Imprint of HarperCollins*Publishers*

Fount Paperbacks is an imprint of
HarperCollins*Religious*
Part of HarperCollins*Publishers*
77-85 Fulham Palace Road, London W6 8JB

First published in Great Britain
in 1990 by Michael Joseph
This edition published 1993
by Fount Paperbacks
3 5 7 9 10 8 6 4 2

A catalogue record for this book
is available from the British Library

ISBN 0 00 627684 9

Printed and bound in Great Britain by
HarperCollinsManufacturing Glasgow

To all the many friends I have made in three decades
of Gilbert and Sullivan

1

It was a splendid funeral. Admittedly there were no funeral orations, hymns at the graveside nor cold ham, pickles or seed cake to follow. This was a church ceremony, simple, but splendidly simple. The only words spoken were the majestic language of the Book of Common Prayer.

'He would not want any fuss,' said the widow, when she made the arrangements. Canon Richard Theophilus Samuel Llewellyn had been a reticent, humourless man. Yet even he might have permitted himself an attempt at a smile over a sentence in the local paper's obituary, 'He was an exhibitionist at his college in Oxford.' Exhibitionism and the vicar of Pontywen were complete strangers.

I had been Curate at Pontywen for barely five months before the sudden death of the parish priest to whom I had come for training after a disastrous first curacy. Those five months had been eventful in the extreme. In that short space of time I had acquired a fiancée, an eccentric colleague and a wealth of parochial experience.

My fiancée was Dr Eleanor Davies, a young lady whose apprenticeship in medicine had forged a common bond with myself, very much an apprentice in holy orders. The catalyst in the forging had been my injured bottom. But that is another story.

The eccentric colleague was Charles Wentworth-Baxter, a clerical misfit thrust upon Canon Llewellyn by the Bishop. Charles, the son of a vicar, had been propelled into his father's footsteps by parental pressure. He seemed destined to be a permanent liability in the priesthood.

Five months in Pontywen had taught me much, partly because

of my vicar's training and partly because of the variety of characters whom I had encountered in this valley parish. From Bertie Owen, the scatterbrained churchwarden of St Padarn's, the daughter church, to Mrs Richards, my landlady, a loveable old lady who could out-Malaprop Mrs Malaprop, Pontywen provided a rich tapestry of humanity.

Now the funeral was over. The Bishop who said the prayers at the committal called me aside in the vestry. He was a scholar and a gentleman. Unfortunately for him and the diocese, he had no knowledge of life in a parish. His background was that of the college quadrangle and the bishop's palace. Furthermore, he was inhibited by a painful shyness.

I remember vividly my first interview with him when I was an ordinand.

'So you are Mr Secombe,' he said after I had been ushered into his presence by his Chaplain.

'Yes, my lord,' I replied nervously.

A long silence ensued during which he looked out of the window opposite him, apparently engrossed in what he saw. It became obvious to me that he was more nervous than I.

I coughed.

He transferred his attention from the window to the papers on his desk.

'You are going to St Matthias for your first curacy, I see,' he remarked. 'You realise it is an evangelical parish.'

'I'm afraid it was the only parish left with a vacancy in the diocese,' I replied.

'I see,' he said and looked out of the window once again. I studied his profile while he studied the window. It was the face of an academic, pale and lean, crowned with silver hair just long enough to intrude upon the back of his coat collar.

It seemed an eternity before he spoke again. I was afraid I had overstepped the mark with my comment. I need not have worried.

'At the moment there is a dearth of vacancies,' he said. 'For the time being you will have to serve the Lord in the parish of St Matthias.'

There followed another hiatus in the conversation, such as it was.

This time I blew my nose.

'Is – er – there anything you wish to ask me?' he enquired.

'No, thank you, my lord,' I replied, only too anxious to save us both further embarrassment.

'In that case, that will be all, Mr Secombe,' he said looking at me for the first and only time in the interview.

Now two and a half years later, the Bishop was about to interview me once again. He was as nervous as ever but this time I felt self assured. Five months in Pontywen had taught me much.

Seated behind the Vicar's desk, in a vestry which was windowless, he chose to study what appeared to be at first sight a large picture of penguins. It was a composite of previous incumbents of Pontywen, over the past ninety-nine years, photographed in the black and white of cassock and surplice.

There was the inevitable silence once the door of the vestry was closed upon the two of us.

Boldly I chose to speak first.

'I hope the arrangements for the funeral were satisfactory,' I said.

To my surprise the Vicar's widow had turned to me for support. She had asked me to take charge of the service, as well as the preparation of the grave which was to be in the churchyard her late husband knew so well.

'Full-Back' Jones, the gravedigger, had excelled himself with the depth of his digging. It was probably the only time he had dug six feet down in the whole of his career as sexton in Pontywen. Mr Matthews the undertaker had conducted proceedings in a manner which rivalled the best of anything which could be offered in Cardiff. What was even more remarkable was the civility between undertaker and gravedigger who were engaged in a private war. There could have been no greater tribute to the memory of Canon Llewellyn than this truce.

The Bishop turned his head away from the clerical penguins and addressed the blotting pad on the Vicar's desk.

'I must say, Mr Secombe,' said the Bishop, 'that the arrangements were impeccable. So much so that I have no hesitation in asking you to – er – take charge of the parish in the interregnum.' He paused.

'That is, of course, with the co-operation of the Rural Dean who is technically in charge of parishes when there is a vacancy.'

Since the Rural Dean was quite content to bury himself in his own rural parish, it was obvious that I would be in sole charge of Pontywen until the arrival of the new Vicar.

'How long will the vacancy last, my lord?' I asked.

'The Board meets in a fortnight's time to make an appointment. If the man nominated accepts, then it will be about another two months or so before he moves in, I should think,' replied the Bishop.

He stood up and shook my hand. The interview was over.

As I left the vestry, 'my bosom swelled with pride' in the words of Sir Joseph Porter in *HMS Pinafore*. For three months I would be in charge of a parish, after little more than two years in holy orders.

The euphoria vanished some minutes later in the Vicarage. I had been invited by the widow to join the post-funeral tea party. It was late October 1945 and the fare was meagre. No black market food had ever crossed the Vicarage threshold. Canon Llewellyn was a man of principle while Mrs Llewellyn was a lady of thrift.

I was consuming a tuna sandwich when I was buttonholed by Dr Elias Hughes, the elderly doctor who had recently appointed my lady love, Eleanor, as his assistant. On the day of Canon Llewellyn's death he had warned me that both he and Eleanor's parents were concerned about our relationship. They felt that she should not begin her medical career and a courtship at the same time. So far I had had no opportunity to speak to Eleanor on the subject.

'A most impressive service, young man,' he said, condescendingly. 'It looks as if you are going to have your hands full for the next few months,' he went on. 'You'll be far too busy to indulge in exchanging sweet nothings with my assistant. Just as well for both of you.'

I was sorely tempted to spread the rest of my tuna sandwich over the old man's countenance.

'This is all I can say to you, Dr Hughes,' I replied in a tone of voice trembling with anger. 'Eleanor and I are responsible adults and we shall decide what is to happen to our relationship.'

I turned away sharply and collided with Charles Wentworth-Baxter who was advancing towards me with a cup of tea in his hand.

Cup and saucer went flying and a shower of tepid tea descended on my best clerical grey suit.

'Ooops!' he exclaimed.

A dozen heads turned in our direction.

'It's quite all right, Mrs Llewellyn,' he said reassuringly. 'Your lovely china is quite intact.'

'What about my carpet?' demanded the widow, her grief in temporary abeyance.

'That's not affected either,' said Charles. 'Fred's suit took the brunt of that.'

'Oh, you two!' she remonstrated. Then she swooped down on the precious china and carried it to safety in the kitchen, tut-tutting throughout the operation.

By now conversation had begun again. Dr Hughes had turned his attention to the Bishop who had retreated behind an arm-chair.

'Sorry, Fred,' murmured my fellow curate.

'So am I,' I replied through clenched teeth.

'I was coming to rescue you from that doctor chap,' he said in a conspiratorial fashion, with his hand planted at the side of his mouth. 'I could see you were getting annoyed.'

'You can say that again,' I replied. 'He was warning me off Eleanor.'

'Never!' gasped Charles.'What a cheek!'

At that moment Mrs Llewellyn emerged from the kitchen with a tea towel which she handed to me.

'Dry your suit with this,' she commanded. Then she rounded on my hapless colleague.

'Trust you to do something stupid,' she said. 'Heaven help the new Vicar when he finds he's got you as his curate.'

So saying she went across the room to rejoin her second cousin who had travelled from Bournemouth for the funeral. She was her only relative present. The others were either dead or uninvited.

'Back to normal,' I commented as I applied the towel to my suit.

'All I hope is that the next Vicar's wife is not like her,' said Charles red faced with embarrassment. 'When I was at my theological college,' he went on, 'our principal used to tell us not to contemplate marriage for some years in case God was calling us to die as missionaries in Africa or in a jungle somewhere. When I look at Mrs Llewellyn I can see the reason why I'd rather be dying in a jungle than married to her.'

'I think I had better get back to my digs and change this suit,' I said. 'Perhaps it won't be permanently stained. The tea was too weak to do that.'

'If you are going,' replied my colleague, 'I'm coming with you. I'm not staying here on my own.'

'Coward,' I whispered.

'It takes a wise man to be a coward,' he retorted.

'In that case,' I said, 'I retract my accusation. You'll never make a coward.'

While he was trying to think out an answer I moved quickly to the widow who was haranguing her cousin.

'Mrs Llewellyn,' I began. 'I'm off back to my digs. I think I had better change my suit.'

Before I could say any more, she launched into another verbal attack on the luckless Charles who had now joined me.

'If you weren't so clumsy, his suit would be intact. But it's too much to expect you to be otherwise.'

She turned to me. 'Thank you for all your help,' she said. 'I'm sure my husband would want me to say that.'

As we left the Vicarage I remarked to Charles, 'I'm not clear whether *she* was thanking me or whether she was acting as a mouthpiece for her late husband.'

'Believe me,' said my fellow curate, 'she is incapable of saying "thank you" any more than she can say "I'm sorry" or "It's not your fault".'

Then we went our separate ways, he to his room over the greengrocer's shop and I to my lodgings at thirteen, Mount Pleasant View.

To my surprise the curtains were drawn in my front room window. They had been open when I left. 'Must be a mark of respect for the late Vicar,' I thought.

To my greater surprise the front door was locked. Mrs Richards, my landlady, had said she would be in when I returned from post-funeral refreshments.

I knocked hard on the door. My landlady was rather deaf. No reply. I knocked so hard again that the knocker was almost wrenched off its hinges.

'Mrs Richards!' I shouted, to the evident interest of a lady with a shopping bag who happened to be passing.

Suddenly there was a slight movement of the curtains in my front room and I had a brief glimpse of Mrs Richards' face. The next minute the door was unbolted and opened a few inches.

'Are there any policemen in the street?' whispered my landlady. 'Not Will Book and Pencil but those ones in plain dress.'

'None that I can see,' I answered. 'Unless they're hiding behind walls or something.'

'Come in quick,' she said.

I slid inside the crack she left open for me. I was under ten stone at that time.

Once I was inside, she slammed the door.

'What's the matter?' I asked. 'Have you got David Matthews inside?' David Matthews had deserted from the army and the police were keeping watch on his parents' house further up the road.

'Of course not!' she exploded. 'As if I would.'

'Well, what is it then?' I demanded.

'It's Miss Jacobs,' she whispered.

Miss Jacobs came to our church and was a generous contributor.

'She's in the middle room,' continued Mrs Richards, 'having a cup of tea while she waits for the police to go.'

'Don't tell me she's a deserter,' I said.

'You're being fastidious,' she replied sternly. 'What it is, is that she's had a tipping up from somebody that the police were going to raid her house this afternoon.'

'Why should the police raid Miss Jacobs' house?' I asked. 'She's a very kind and generous lady.'

'Didn't the Vicar ever tell you about her?' she said.

'Tell me what?' I replied, more than a little bewildered.

'She's a turf counter, a booktaker, you know, taking bets on horses and things. She's been caught twice and had to pay a lot of money. You'd better come in and say hello. Perhaps you could revive her, she needs it poor thing. I was just on my way to the poor Vicar's funeral when she came to me for subterfuge.'

We went into the middle room where Miss Jacobs was seated at the table which was covered with Mrs Richards' best lace tablecloth on which reposed a teapot, adorned with the best tea-cosy, the best cups and saucers and the aptly named homemade rock-cakes on the best tea plate. Miss Jacobs was a desiccated spinster of fifty years or so, whose bird-like nose sported a pair of pince-nez. She was more like a schoolteacher than an illegal turf accountant.

'Trouble, Miss Jacobs?' I said, sounding like her grandfather rather than her junior.

Her sallow face flushed into a colour more akin to an orange than a beetroot.

'The law is an ass, young man,' she said. Irked by my condescension, she sounded like a schoolteacher. 'It's all right for the rich to have their pleasure, but the poor can't have theirs without the police interfering. Somebody came in and said they'd seen the police were on their way up the street. I had no time to hide the betting slips so I just locked the door and ran up here with them to Mrs Richards. I knew she'd help me. Once the coast is clear, as it were, I'll go back home and lie low for

8

a time. I'll have to have a word with Ike and Llew.'

'Who are Ike and Llew?' I asked innocently.

'My runners, of course!' she replied impatiently. 'There are two kinds of runners, young man, the horses and the bookies' collectors. Ike and Llew collect the slips and the money for me. Most of that comes in twopenny doubles not pound notes.'

'In that case,' I said, 'I know one of your best customers – Full-Back Jones the gravedigger. At least I take it that he's one of your clientele. I wondered where he went to place his bets.'

She glared at me. 'I never divulge the names of my punters, Mr Secombe, any more than you would disclose confidences passed on to you by your parishioners.'

'My apologies, Miss Jacobs,' I replied. 'You are obviously a lady of principle.'

'Goodness me!' exclaimed Mrs Richards who had become aware of the accident to my suit. 'What has happened to you? Your bit of best is in a state. It's all miscoloured.'

'A cup of tea was spilt over me,' I explained. 'Charles Wentworth-Baxter collided with me. It wasn't his fault. I turned quickly and banged into him.'

'Just like him,' snorted my landlady. 'He's like a bear in a Chinese shop. Go up and change and I'll see what I can do to it when Miss Jacobs has gone.'

I was grateful for the opportunity to escape to the privacy of my bedroom. Dr Hughes' remarks were still echoing in my ears. I needed to see Eleanor as soon as possible to find out if she had been warned off our relationship. There had been no chance for us to meet since the Vicar's sudden death.

As I divested myself of my trousers and stood in my shirt and underpants, there was a loud banging on the front door. This was followed by stealthy footsteps up the staircase.

'Get inside the wardrobe,' panted old Mrs Richards at the top of the stairs.

My door was flung open to reveal a wide-eyed Miss Jacobs.

'Not that door,' whispered my landlady somewhat belatedly, 'the next one.' My door was shut and the other door opened in a split second.

Now the knocker was used with even greater vigour.

I slipped on my discarded trousers and made my way down

the stairs. Bracing myself to confront the arm of the law, I opened the door slowly.

Standing in front of me, in filthy raincoat and wellingtons, with his even filthier trilby on his head, was the figure of Full-Back Jones.

His unshaven face split in a toothless grimace.

'Caught you,' he said.

'What do you mean "caught me"?' I answered with as much dignity as I could muster, standing there in my trousers, shirt and braces.

'I went to the Vicarage and they said you was back 'ome,' said the gravedigger. 'Sorry I disturbed you just as you was going to 'ave a lie down.'

'Excuse me, I was not going to have "a lie down", as you say.' My hackles had risen. 'I was changing my suit. Now what can I do for you?'

He was taken aback by my reaction. His grin vanished to be replaced by a look of solicitude, as if I was sickening for measles or something.

'Hold on, boss,' he murmured. 'I've only come to ask if you wants them wreaths left at the side of the grave or on top when I've finished filling it in. I'm going 'ome for my tea now.'

By now my anger had subsided. I was relieved it was only Full-Back Jones instead of the law.

'Sorry to snap your head off,' I said. 'I've had a trying day.'

He nodded in sympathy.

'I'm sure it will look better if you put the flowers on top of the grave, once you've filled it in.'

'Righto, boss,' he said, grinning once again. 'I'll see to that. Don't worry, I'll make a good job of tidying the grave. He wasn't such a bad old – er – boyo. Be seeing you.'

I closed the door and shouted 'It's all right. You can come down now. It was only Full-Back Jones.' In no time at all I had bounded upstairs.

The first to emerge from the bedroom was Mrs Richards, clutching her bosom.

'What a fright!' she breathed. 'I was sure it was the CDI and we'd all have been up in front of the Judge and those jury people.'

A few seconds later Miss Jacobs emerged from the room

looking distinctly embarrassed, her pince-nez almost on the end of her nose.

Pausing at the top of the stairs, she said to me, 'I'm so sorry to have caused all this trouble. Mrs Richards and you have been very kind. I think the time has come for me to go back to my house.'

A few minutes later as I was changing into my second-best suit, I heard the front door opening and Mrs Richards speeding the parting guest.

'I'm making us a fresh cup of tea,' said my landlady, when I arrived downstairs. 'We'll need it to reprocicate.'

'We shall indeed,' I replied. 'I must say it was very noble of you to shelter Miss Jacobs, especially since it meant you missing the Vicar's funeral.'

'First things first,' said the old lady. 'She was on my doorstep and I couldn't turn her away. As the Bible says, cast your bread on the waterfall and you'll get it back seventy times seven. Look what she's left for you.'

She handed me a five pound note, more than my pay for a month. I stared at it in amazement, I had never seen a note of that magnitude.

'What a wonderful waterfall,' I gasped. 'I don't know whether to frame this or spend it.'

'It's no use to you stuck on the wall, like a Muriel. Why don't you and your young lady have a night out in Cardiff with a slapped up meal and things?'

'That's a splendid suggestion Mrs Richards. Do you know that Dr Hughes told me again today to keep away from her.'

'She's the kind of little girl who will do what she wants to do. No Dr Hughes is going to stand in *her* shadow, believe me.'

'I hope you're right,' I said fervently.

'I'm sure I'm right,' insisted Mrs Richards. 'Now can I have your suit, please?'

2

Next morning when I came down to breakfast Mrs Richards handed me an envelope.

'I found this on the doormat,' she said. 'It's for you with no stamp on. It's either a late bird or an early worm has brought it because it wasn't here when I went to bed.'

There was a faint suggestion of perfume exuding from the dainty, pink envelope. I recognised Eleanor's writing at first glance. It was addressed to 'The Reverend Frederick Thomas Secombe, BA, Acting Vicar.'

Inside was a short note, 'Fred, my dear, please excuse this scribble. I'm writing this on my knee, in the front seat of the car, by the light of a street lamp. We must meet. See you outside St Padarn's at 6.30 p.m. after surgery. Eleanor. PS. Delivering this at 2 a.m. after delivering nine pounds of baby. PPS. I.L.Y.'

'This was brought by a late bird, Mrs Richards,' I announced.

'Well, it's one with good news by the look on your face,' she commented.

'Couldn't be better,' I burbled. 'It's from Eleanor. She wants to meet me tonight.'

'Some more good news for you,' said my landlady. 'I've got those tide marks out of your best suit. So you'll be able to meet your financée looking very smart.'

Later in the morning Charles Wentworth-Baxter arrived for a parish management meeting I had arranged. With three churches to look after, the months ahead would be both time consuming and harassing. Suddenly I was aware that a Vicar's lot was not an easy one. With only two curates and a lay reader to perform the duties, making out a rota for Sunday services would be a headache. Baptisms, marriages, Sunday School, sick visiting, pastoral visiting, parish organisations – the list of chores seemed endless. To that list I had added another, the Church Gilbert and Sullivan group.

The late Vicar had given me permission, somewhat grudgingly, to form a Gilbert and Sullivan company. They had had their first rehearsal less than a week ago. With the help of Eleanor I had managed to enlist the services of the music master at the local grammar school and some of his female pupils. Charles had undertaken the duties of the accompanist very competently. Eleanor had a delightful soprano voice and had taken the lead in a number of Savoy Operas. We had seemed set for an untroubled passage ahead of *The Pirates of Penzance*. With the death of Canon Llewellyn, however, there could be squalls if the new Vicar turned out to be Father John Whittaker.

As we sat in the front room of thirteen, Mount Pleasant View, life assumed a very complicated pattern. On the one hand there was Charles, my colleague, who was incapable of taking a service on his own, on the other there was Ezekiel Evans, the lay reader who thought he was capable of taking any service on his own. His congregations suffered from inordinately long sermons and from his inability to cope with his aitches. With helpers like these, the immediate future looked like a disaster area.

In front of me on the table was a blank sheet of paper, flaunting itself. It had remained inviolate for half an hour.

'Well, we must make a start,' I announced. 'We have been talking all this time without getting anywhere. The first thing to do is to put Ezekiel Evans out in the sticks in Llanhyfryd.'

'Old Inasmuch,' commented Charles.

'Old who?' I asked.

'Ezekiel Evans,' he replied. 'Haven't you noticed his favourite word? It comes out every other sentence.'

'You mean "h'inasmuch",' I said. 'Inasmuch as he bores everybody to death, the fewer people he can afflict the better. So out to the rustics he goes. That leaves the parish church and St Padarn's.'

'Can't we stagger the times so that we can take the services together in both churches?' pleaded my fellow curate.

'Not on your nelly,' I said firmly. 'There would be an uprising in no time. I'm afraid, Charles, that your hour of destiny has arrived. From now on you will have to stand on your own two feet.'

He turned pale and stared at me as if I had ordered him to go on a Kamikaze mission.

'The best thing to do,' I continued, 'is to put you down for the Communion service in St Padarn's. Bertie Owen will take care of you, believe me. Then you can come to the parish church in the evening. It will be evensong. So you won't have to cope with the Communion service there. I'll go to St Padarn's in the evening. I must go there once a Sunday – especially since I am supposed to be in charge of it.'

'But what about all the other things?' asked Charles in plaintive tones. 'Weddings, baptisms and all that?'

'We'll leave that till next Monday. There's nothing fixed for this weekend as far as I know,' I replied loftily.

'And don't forget we're supposed to have that Gilbert and Sullivan rehearsal tomorrow,' my colleague reminded me. 'I've been practising the music on Mrs Howells' piano. She's got a nice contralto voice, by the way.'

Myfanwy Howells, the local greengrocer's wife, was Charles's landlady.

Over the midday meal my landlady and I discussed Mrs Llewellyn's plight.

'It must be terrible for her,' commented Mrs Richards. 'She's got no real friends nor relatives by the sound of it. She must feel like Robertson Caruso on that desert island. I feel very sorry for her even though she's a crick in the neck.'

'So do I,' I replied. 'I never thought I would but she was so helpless after the Vicar's death. She was only too glad to let me take charge of the arrangements.'

'And very good they were too,' she said. 'You'll have to do the same for me when I'm diseased.'

'I hope that won't be for a long time yet. You've got a lot of life left in you still,' I assured her. 'Anyway, I'd better go and see her later this afternoon. I want to go through the list of baptisms and weddings the Vicar had arranged and any other information I can get.'

'Yes,' said Mrs Richards, 'he was very methodistical. All the curates said that even if they didn't like him.'

The widow looked genuinely pleased to see me when I went

to the Vicarage. She showed me into the lounge which reeked of furniture polish and beckoned me into one of the armchairs.

'Thank you for all your help,' she began. 'I'm afraid I didn't know where to start. The Canon always saw to any arrangements that had to be made.'

She never used his Christian name. I wondered whether even in their most intimate relations, if they ever had any, she would still address him as Canon.

'By the way,' she went on, pointing at the carpet, 'I managed to get the stains out where Wentworth-Baxter spilt that cup of tea.'

'You'll be pleased to know, Mrs Llewellyn,' I replied, 'that Mrs Richards has got the stains out of my suit.'

'Oh, of course, it went over your suit as well, didn't it?' she said with a sigh. 'What a stupid man he is.'

'As I said yesterday if you remember, it was more my fault than his.' My remark was made so firmly that she dropped the subject forthwith.

'Would you like a cup of tea, Mr Secombe?' she asked.

While she was in the kitchen I stood up and looked out of the French windows at the lawn. It looked a picture of cloisteral calm.

Suddenly the Vicarage gate opened and Bertie Owen, the churchwarden from St Padarn's appeared. Tall, upright, he marched purposefully down the drive. Halfway down he stopped and stared at the side of the house which adjoined the garage.

With his head to one side, he walked slowly on tiptoes, pausing occasionally, as if he were a cat stalking its prey. Past the windows he went. Next minute there was one almighty shout from Bertie, 'Got you!'

There followed a series of muffled expostulations. Into sight hove Bertie, his trilby over his eyes and his two arms locked around the throat of a little man, with a cap and muffler surmounting his dark grey raincoat.

I ran to the front door and opened it. There was the churchwarden, as pleased as punch, like our cat at home presenting a dead sparrow on the doorstep.

'A citizen's arrest,' he announced. 'This man was attempting to break into the garage and steal the Vicar's car.'

15

The alleged criminal lifted his head. His bespectacled eyes met mine. They were not those of a criminal caught in the act, but of an innocent, full of righteous indignation. What is more, they belonged to a pompous innocent, a very pompous innocent, the Vicar of Abertrisant, Father John Whittaker.

'Tell this idiot who I am,' he hissed through his closed dentures.

Bertie's hands dropped to his sides.

'This is the Vicar of Abertrisant,' I said.

The citizen's mouth and eyes opened wide. He stood speechless.

'What on earth did you think you were doing, Bertie?' I demanded.

'Well,' he began, 'I was working six till two this morning so I thought I'd come and see if there was anything I could do to help Mrs Llewellyn this afternoon. Then when I was coming down the drive, I saw this man, I beg your pardon, this Vicar, trying to look inside the garage. I knew the Vicar's car would be in there and I suspected he was after it.'

He turned to the little man who was still purple with anger.

'I'm very sorry, Vicar, but you see, you didn't look like a Vicar with that cap and scarf *and* you've got a collar and tie on.' He pointed at the layman's attire which was now revealed.

His explanation did little to soothe Father Whittaker.

'You could at least have checked who I was first,' he shouted. 'Do I look like a burglar?'

'Not now,' replied Bertie. 'But you did then.'

At this stage of the conversation Mrs Llewellyn appeared from the kitchen, alerted by the shouting at the open door.

She stared at the Vicar of Abertrisant. It was one of her hostile specials. It was less than a week since she had told me that she feared he would like to come to Pontywen and that she found him obnoxious.

'What are you doing here?' she demanded.

The purple on Father Whittaker's face was transformed into an off-white.

'I – er – thought I'd come and have a look around as I – er – happened to be passing. I was about to come to the front door after I'd had a look at the garage when I was apprehended by this idiot.'

Bertie was unabashed.

'Mrs Llewellyn,' he said, 'he was by the garage trying to open the door and with his cap and scarf of course I thought he was a burglar.'

'Well done,' replied the widow. 'Perhaps you'd like to come in and join Mr Secombe for a cup of tea.'

Bertie strutted in, proud as a peacock.

The Vicar's purple returned.

'As for you, Mr Whittaker,' he winced at the 'Mr', 'you might have waited another week or so before coming to spy out the land. Next time perhaps you will knock at the front door first.'

With that she closed the door with such a bang that it thundered through the hall.

'Go on into the sitting room with Mr Secombe,' she commanded and went into the kitchen.

'You were lucky it was John Whittaker you got hold of, Bertie,' I told him. 'If it were any other person, Mrs Llewellyn would not have treated you to a cup of tea. You would have been treated to the sharp edge of her tongue. All I hope, for your sake as well as mine, is that he does not get appointed to this parish.'

'After being shop steward for the past four years and churchwarden at St Padarn's for the past ten years,' said Bertie nonchalantly, 'I think I can deal with him if that happens. He's only five foot nothing anyway.'

'So was Napoleon,' I replied, 'and he conquered half of Europe. What's more, John Whittaker is convinced he is Napoleon.'

'In that case,' riposted Bertie, 'he'd better go and see one of those mental doctors. It's all the loopy cases who think they're Napoleon. Old Mr Bevan from Balaclava Street, when he went demented, thought he was Lord Kitchener because he had a moustache like him. He used to go out into the street in his nightshirt, pointing at everybody and shouting "Your country needs you".'

The entry of Mrs Llewellyn with the tray of light refreshments ended any further discussion about the connection between Father John Whittaker, Napoleon and Lord Kitchener. She was still fuming about the indelicacy of a fellow priest intruding into

17

the privacy of a widow less than a week after her husband's death.

'To think he might come here and undo all that the Canon had built up over thirty years,' she said bitterly.

'I tell you one thing, Mrs Llewellyn,' asserted Bertie forcefully. 'He'd better not try it on in St Padarn's. I've helped to organise strikes at the works. I'll organise one in our church if it's necessary.'

'That will be interesting,' I said.

'You wait,' boasted Bertie.

After the cup of tea and a digestive biscuit Mrs Llewellyn allowed me into the Vicar's study to rummage through his filing cabinet. Meanwhile, Bertie had been let loose in the garden.

The late Canon Llewellyn was a methodical parish priest. Every street in Pontywen was documented with the names and details of church families with remarks in a wide column. These varied from 'Once a year Xian' to the five-star Christians 'weekly communicants, good givers'.

There were three weddings fixed for November and December and four baptisms for the second Sunday in November. For some strange reason, Canon Llewellyn chose the second Sunday in the month for his baptisms. I made a note of the weddings and christenings and arranged with Mrs Llewellyn that all callers at the Vicarage should be referred to me at thirteen, Mount Pleasant View.

On my way down the Vicarage drive, Bertie Owen darted from behind a magnolia tree, secateurs in hand.

'Do you know if you've got to prune these mangolias?' he enquired.

'I haven't the faintest idea,' I answered. 'And if I were you I wouldn't prune anything. Just gather up the autumn leaves and make a bonfire or something, but ask Mrs Llewellyn before you do any pruning.'

The suggestion about a bonfire caught his fancy.

'I'll have a word with her,' he said, 'after I've got to work on the bonfire. See you Sunday.'

'By the way,' I told him, 'Charles Wentworth-Baxter will be with you for the Communion service. So take care of him, I'll be there at evensong.'

'Don't worry, Mr Secombe,' replied Bertie. 'I'll look after him.'

Back at my lodgings I told my landlady about Bertie's apprehension of the clerical burglar.

'That Vicar shouldn't have been acting like a creeping Tom,' she said. 'It's his own fault.'

'What I'm afraid of,' I replied, 'is that he might be made Vicar of Pontywen.'

'If "ifs" and "ans" were made of pots and pans you'd have to shoot for bacon,' pronounced Mrs Richards. 'In any case, he won't be coming for a few months. So you make hail while the sun shines.'

Buoyed by my landlady's philosophy, I ventured forth later on to meet Eleanor as she had suggested in her note outside St Padarn's Church.

The lamp outside the church gate was not functioning. I arrived in total darkness to await the arrival of my love in her old Morris Minor. Eventually the noise of a large sewing machine in the distance signalled her approach. The headlights beamed out from the corner of Taliesin Road adjacent to the church and then swung round to put me in the spotlight.

'What can ail thee, knight at arms, alone and palely loitering,' quoted Eleanor through the open window of the car. 'Hop in, mate.'

I hopped in and attempted an immediate embrace which was foiled by the handbrake.

'Hold on, you impetuous cleric!' she exclaimed. 'We'll drive out into the country and get into the back seat. In the meanwhile hold your horses.'

'Any chance of coming for a meal somewhere?' I enquired. 'I've been given a five pound note and it's burning a hole in my pocket.'

'It will have to smoulder for a few days, my dear,' she said. 'As you are probably aware, I am redolent of antiseptic, not Chanel Number Five. Pardon my inquisitiveness, but how did you come to acquire a five pound note?'

'From a bookie,' I replied.

'There's no need to tell lies,' she remonstrated. 'And you a curate. You should be ashamed of yourself.'

'It's true,' I insisted. 'If you drive on to our next stopping place, I'll tell you the whole story after I've had my way with you.'

'What with talk about bookies and having your way with me, Fred Secombe, you are becoming totally corrupt. I shall have to clamp down on these tendencies.' She put her foot down on the accelerator and the noisy old vehicle carried us off into a country lane some three or four miles away.

After the noise of the engine, the silence of the countryside was intense.

'Shall we get in the back seat?' I whispered.

'Why are you whispering?' Eleanor demanded in a loud voice.

'It's so quiet,' I murmured.

'For heaven's sake, let's get in the back seat,' she said. 'And don't forget it's only kisses and cuddles.'

'I was only joking,' I replied.

'Joking and hoping, you mean. You can have your way with me when we've got a piece of paper with written permission. Till then, my love, carry on cuddling.'

I did that and very satisfactory it was.

'Now then,' she said some time later. 'What's all this about a bookie?'

I told her the story about Miss Jacobs.

'Didn't you know she was a bookmaker?' she asked. 'I could have told you that. You really are an innocent abroad. However, we have more important things to discuss, like Dr Hughes, for example.'

'So he's had words with you as well as with me,' I said. 'I told him that our relationship had nothing to do with him. What worries me is that you might lose your post. He also informed me that your parents were perturbed by our romance, if one may call it that.'

'One may indeed call it that, my dear,' she replied quietly and kissed me. 'First of all, well done, you, that you stood up to old Hughes. He needs me too much to get rid of me. I have told him that my private affairs are none of his business. As for my parents, I have been equally firm with them. I'm a big girl now and I can make up my own mind. I wanted to see you to stop you worrying. Before long I shall have to take you to meet my parents. Once they realise what a catch you are, that will end any opposition from them.'

'I hardly think I come into the category of a catch,' I said. 'Brought up on a council estate in Swansea, a penniless curate.'

'What do you mean "penniless"?' she replied. 'A man with a five pound note burning a hole in his pocket! As for being brought up on a council estate, my father was brought up in a miner's cottage. So don't have any delusions about my origins. In any case, it isn't a man's background that makes him a catch, it's his character and his abilities.'

'The Lord is gracious unto Zion,' I intoned.

She stared at me.

'In other words,' I said, 'God has been very kind, sending me such a delightful little parcel of happiness.'

'My dear Frederick,' she replied, 'this little parcel had better get home to its dinner because its inside is empty. I'm starving. I'll be seeing you tomorrow evening anyway at the G and S rehearsal. We'll fix up a date to spend some of your five pounds.'

So saying she kissed me ardently once more and then made a quick transference to the driving seat. A quarter of an hour later she was dropping me outside my digs.

The light was on in my room downstairs and the curtains were drawn. As soon as I opened the front door, Bertie Owen made a rapid appearance from my sanctum, his suit dishevelled and his face looking as if he had just finished a stint at the deep level in the colliery.

'They've put it out now,' he announced excitedly. 'The Vicarage is OK. It's only the garage and the Vicar's car.'

'Calm down, Bertie,' I said. 'Then tell me what it's all about.'

'Well,' he began, 'you told me to gather up all the leaves and make a bonfire. So I asked Mrs Llewellyn for a rake and I got a big mound of leaves together, down by the garage.'

'Say no more,' I said. 'Why didn't you make the bonfire at the top of the drive?'

'The point was,' he went on, 'that I started up there and then worked down to the garage. It's easier working downhill than uphill. Anyway, when I'd got a decent lot of leaves and twigs together I decided to light the fire. The leaves weren't very dry so I used a petrol can I found by the garage. There seemed like only a drop in the can. I tipped it up on the bonfire. There was more in it than I thought and there was a big 'oosh! It's a wonder I didn't catch fire myself. Next minute the flames got hold of the garage. I ran to Mrs Llewellyn and she phoned the fire brigade. I got buckets of water but it was too fierce. In the end the firemen came and put out the fire. The garage is gone and the Vicar's car but everything else is fine.'

'Bertie,' I said, 'why didn't I tell you to carry on pruning? It would have been less expensive. Is Mrs Llewellyn all right?'

'She's very annoyed,' he replied, 'but apart from that she's – er . . .'

'Fine, like everything else,' I interjected.

'That's right, Mr Secombe,' he said. 'Mind, I don't mind telling you she called me a few names.'

'I'm sure she did,' I replied. 'You must like spectacular fires. Remember your effort on VJ Day when you set all the fireworks off at once.'

'Ah, that was an accident,' said Bertie.

'What was this tonight?' I asked.

'There's a difference between garden leaves and fireworks,' he replied indignantly.

'Bertie, thank you for your help,' I said. 'I think you'd better go home to Mrs Owen. She'll be wondering where you are.'

'That's what I'm afraid of,' he muttered and made his way slowly out through the door into the night.

3

'I'd better go round to the Vicarage and see Mrs Llewellyn,' I said to Mrs Richards at breakfast. 'In a sense I am responsible for the fire. I shouldn't have stopped Bertie using the secateurs. He might have destroyed a few bushes perhaps. As it is he has destroyed a garage and a car.'

'You can never forthtell the future,' the old lady replied. 'Bertie Owen is a law with himself. Sometimes I've listened with blanket astonishment when people say what he's done.'

'That's what I mean,' I said.

Mrs Llewellyn greeted me at the Vicarage door with a frown so intense that her eyebrows seemed to be tied in a knot.

'Have you heard?' she snapped.

'Indeed I have. Bertie came round to tell me last night.'

'Don't mention that fool's name to me. Just come and see what damage he's done. Fancy lighting a fire by a wooden shed.'

She swept out of the house and led me round to the side where once was a garage and a car. The building had disappeared and standing in a carpet of ashes was a metal skeleton. On either side of the departed shed were trees, now 'bared, ruin'd choirs where late the sweet birds sang'.

'The firemen said it was providential that the petrol tank in the car was almost empty. Otherwise it might have been even worse. Why on earth the idiot decided to sweep up the leaves when he had said he was going to prune some of the bushes, I don't know.' She shook her head in bewilderment.

I refrained from supplying the answer.

'You'd better come in.' It was more of a command than an invitation.

The clergy widow's face was pale and drawn. It was obvious

that the events of the past week had taken their toll. She ushered me into the lounge, beckoned me into an armchair and sank down on the settee opposite me.

'I'll be so glad to leave this place now,' she said, reinforcing her words with a deep sigh. 'What with that dreadful man Whittaker snooping around and then the fire. All on top of the Canon's death coming out of the blue. It's, it's too much.' She fought back the tears.

Suddenly I felt intensely sorry for the woman. The stony exterior was crumbling and a human being was emerging, lonely and unloved.

'Is there anything I can do, Mrs Llewellyn?' I enquired solicitously, anxious to atone for the fire.

'Not at the moment but thank you all the same. You have been very helpful.' I winced. Mrs Llewellyn blew her nose. 'I think I've got a cold coming on,' she said. 'Whatever happens, I shall be out of the house as soon as possible.'

'That means,' I said to myself as I went down the Vicarage drive, 'a new Vicar in Pontywen in less than no time.' Clergy widows were allowed to stay in the Vicarage or Rectory for a maximum of three months. After that they were expected to leave what had been their home for many years and to find accommodation elsewhere, blessed with a paltry pension and whatever savings had been scraped together. If a vicar's lot was not an easy one a clergy widow's lot was much worse. Mrs Llewellyn's future was going to be a grim one. Because of her imminent departure, it might be that my future would be equally grim very soon if Father John Whittaker arrived in Pontywen.

To take my mind off such a fate, I decided to spend the afternoon visiting some of the faithful who worshipped at the parish church, using the list I had obtained from the Vicarage study. First on the sheet in my parson's notebook was Mrs Greenfield, the organist's wife, described in the late Vicar's words as 'regular churchgoer, neurotic'.

It was a blustery autumn day. The Greenfields lived in one of the streets on the top of the hill near the hospital, Sebastopol Terrace. I knocked at the door of number ten. The brass knocker gleamed in the watery sunshine. There was no reply. I knocked once more, to no avail, it seemed. As I was about to move away, the door slowly opened to reveal a little woman, thin and bespectacled. She was wearing an immaculately clean pinafore over her dress. Her sparse grey hair was in curlers. Her eyes were reddened with weeping.

'Come in quickly, Mr Secombe,' she said, 'before that old dust blows in here.'

I was taken into the front room where the brass fender gleamed like the knocker. Family photographs adorned the mantelpiece. I sat down in the armchair by the window where a large aspidistra reposed on a stand. Suddenly she produced a duster from a pocket in her pinafore and advanced upon the armchair, flicking dust off the polished Rexine.

'Excuse me,' she breathed. 'I can't stand to see dust.'

Then she retired to the settee where she continued her search for any speck of dust which had dared to defy her. After satisfying herself that her furniture was one hundred per cent unsullied, she turned her attention to me.

'I'm so glad you've called at this moment, Mr Secombe.' Mrs Greenfield paused and produced a handkerchief from the other pocket. Tears began to pour down her face only to be wiped away as quickly as the dust on the furniture.

'There's been a terrible tragedy this morning.' Pause for more tears and vigorous wiping.

'You've had a bereavement, I can see. Not Mr Greenfield surely?'

'No, of course not. He's just gone back to work at the office. He did all he could but it was no use, no use at all.'

My bewilderment was growing with her every sentence.

'I suppose we have been bereaved in a way,' she went on. 'I know he wasn't a human being but he was just as dear to us as if he was. He was a part of the family. Billie's been with us for five years and now he's gone.' The tears began to flow again. Her handkerchief had become a sodden ball of cotton.

'I'm so sorry, Mrs Greenfield,' I murmured. 'I know how attached you can become to a dog.'

'Billie wasn't a dog,' she said indignantly. 'He was our budgie. I used to let him out of his cage to stretch his wings. He'd land on my shoulder and nibble my ear and things. He could say "My name is Billie Greenfield". Not any more he can't and it's my fault. I should have shut the kitchen door.' She wailed loudly and then began to sob uncontrollably.

I decided not to venture on another comment. So I sat, staring at the carpet, trying to think of an excuse to leave the house of mourning.

Suddenly the crying ceased. I looked up to see Mrs Greenfield making a determined attempt to keep a rein on herself.

'I'm sorry, Mr Secombe, to go on like this,' she bit her lip and paused. 'He was flying around in the middle room and then came out into the kitchen where I was cooking the chips for my husband's dinner. "Go away Billie," I said and waved my arm. I – I hit him accidentally and he fell into the chip pan. It was awful.' Another bout of tears ensued.

'I can see why you're upset,' I said, fighting hard to contain my inconvenient sense of humour.

'Thank you, Mr Secombe, for your sympathy. But nothing will bring him back. I got him out of the pan with a tablespoon and laid him on the table by the gas stove. His little legs were stuck up in the air and I tried to give him the mouth to mouth resuscitation. It was no use, he'd gone – for ever.'

My facial muscles began to ache from an overdose of control.

'When my husband came home for his dinner, I got him to wrap the poor thing in one of my best doylies and bury him at the bottom of the garden. He's at peace there now and he can hear the other birds singing up above him. Or perhaps he's in heaven. Do you believe there are budgies in heaven, Mr Secombe?'

I swallowed hard.

'Well, Mrs Greenfield,' I said, 'that's something I haven't thought about until now. There's nothing about it in the New Testament, I know that. Still, after all, they are God's creatures and you never know.'

This seemed to reassure her.

'It would be nice to think he's up there waiting for me when I go.'

Two cups of tea later, I left number ten Sebastopol Street, only too pleased that I had not been asked to say a few prayers over the victim's grave.

The rest of the afternoon's visiting was uneventful. I arrived at my digs with an interior drenched with tea and with an urgent desire to drain it. As I rushed into the middle room on my way to the outside lavatory, I was confronted by Mrs Richards.

'There's two people in the front room.'

Before she could say any more I had sprinted to the safety of the 'ty bach', as they say in Wales, 'the little house'.

On my return, my landlady met me. 'My word, Mr Secombe, you were in extremities, weren't you?'

'I'm sorry to be rude,' I said. 'I had far too much tea to drink once again. You were saying that I have two visitors.'

'Yes. One of them is Gloria May Thomas. She's getting married in a fortnight's time, she says. A real gibberty filbert, that one. The other is Zekiel Evans coming about Sunday, I think.'

'Would you mind if one of them waited in the middle room?'

'That Gloria May was first in and she wants to get home. She's come straight from the factory.'

'In that case, perhaps you'd look after Ezekiel Evans.'

'It's Dobson's choice, I suppose,' sighed Mrs Richards.

I met a wall of silence as I went into the front room. Gloria May and Ezekiel were sitting on the edge of their chairs, she clad in overalls, her hair hidden under a scarf, and he in his black pinstripe suit, nursing a trilby. Both glared at me, daring me to make the wrong order of preference.

'Mr Evans,' I said and smiled wanly, 'would you care to enjoy Mrs Richards' company for a few minutes while I deal with the young lady? I'd like to have a chat with you.'

He stood up, clearly affronted.

'H'I'm afraid, it will 'ave to be a few words not a chat h'inasmuch as h'I've got to be 'ome for tea by 'alf past five. It's ten past now.'

'I've got to get the fish and chips for the family. They'll be waiting for their meal.' Gloria May's eyes were blazing.

'In that case, I shan't keep either of you more than a few minutes.'

Ezekiel stalked out of the room, closing the door with unnecessary vigour.

'That man,' snorted Gloria May. 'I don't know who 'e do think 'e is. 'E lives in our street but you'd think he lived in Bucking'am Palace the way 'e is.'

'You're getting married,' I said.

'That's why I've come. To find out what's 'appening with the old Vicar dead an' that. I booked the wedding provisional three months ago. My boy-friend is in the army so I've got to do everything myself, and my father's in the army, too.'

'Don't worry. Everything is in hand. Come and see me a week tomorrow at half-past seven.' I produced another sickly smile.

'Is that all? I needn't 'ave wasted my time coming.' So saying she swept out of the room and was out through the front door in less time than I took to get to the 'ty bach'.

I drew a deep breath and went into the middle room where the lay reader was standing like the statue of the Marquess of Bute in the centre of Cardiff with one hand on the table and the other across his middle.

'OK, Mr Evans,' I said, 'shall we retire to the front room?'

He grunted and followed me into my sanctum.

'H'if you don't mind, h'I won't be seated. H'I'll come straight to the point. H'I gather you 'ave harranged for me to take the service in Llan'yfryd. 'Ow ham h'I supposed to get there?' His finger stabbed the air in my direction.

'Good point,' I commented. The question of transport had slipped my mind. 'I could ask Bertie Owen to lend you his bicycle.'

'H'I'm afraid h'I've never mounted a bicycle. In any case h'I suffer from vertigo.'

'It's not a penny-farthing, Mr Evans, nor a bucking bronco. I had to learn how to ride it.'

'You don't 'ave to be sarcastic, young man. H'I'm not going to start riding a bicycle h'at my age.'

'There's only one thing for it. You'll have to go by taxi. Those farmers in Llanhyfryd will have to pay the cost out of the collection. Tell them I say so.'

'They won't like that, you know 'ow tight fisted they are. H'inasmuch h'as you are not the Vicar, they won't like it, h'I can tell you.'

'The Bishop has placed me in charge until the new Vicar comes. You can tell them that, Mr Evans.'

'Very well. H'I'll see Jones the taxi people tonight but, believe me, there'll be h'any amount of trouble about this.'

I told Mrs Richards about my encounters with Mr Evans and Gloria May.

'That Gloria May has always been a crick in the neck,' she said. 'As for old Zekiel Evans I wouldn't give fourpence for what he thinks. Forget them, Mr Secombe and enjoy your tea.'

I followed her instructions and went on my way to the second Gilbert and Sullivan rehearsal whistling the waltz tune 'Poor Wandering One' from *The Pirates of Penzance*.

Charles had already opened up by the time I arrived there and was practising the piano accompaniment for the rehearsal. For someone who was not too keen on his pastoral work he was very enthusiastic about this theatrical venture of mine.

'What about casting this opera?' he asked.

'Hold on, Charles,' I said, 'there's plenty of time for that. I'm sure more people will join us once the word gets round Pontywen that we're doing *Pirates*.'

Right on cue entered a big burly red-faced man in his forties.

'Is this where they are starting a musical society to do a show?' He had a deep rich bass voice.

'It certainly is,' I replied and advanced on him holding out my hand. He shook it with a grip like a vice.

'My name is Islwyn Jenkins. I'm farming up in Llanhyfryd. I've done a bit of singing and a bit of fooling around but I don't know anything about Gilbert and Sullivan.'

'Neither do most of the others who joined last week. So you're in good company. Pleased to have you with us anyway. I'm Fred Secombe and this is Charles Wentworth-Baxter.'

Charles examined his fingers after the handshake, as if they had been put out of action for the rest of the evening.

Very soon last week's contingent trooped in, led by Aneurin Williams, the musical director, with girls from his school.

There was no sign of Eleanor when the rehearsal began. By the time Aneurin had halted proceedings for a ten minute break I was in a mental turmoil. A dozen scenarios accounting for her absence had raced through my mind, ranging from a car accident to an almighty row with her parents. It was time for action, I felt. A phone call was necessary.

'I'm just going to make a phone call,' I said to Aneurin.

'OK, Mr Secombe. I've been wondering where she is, myself.'

As I emerged from the hall into the Stygian gloom outside, I could hear a car groaning its way up the hill. Seconds later it accelerated into the flat stretch of road and pulled up outside St Padarn's with a screech of brakes.

Eleanor had arrived.

She was out of the car in a trice, with the score of *Pirates* under her arm. I advanced on her and gave her an enormous bear hug.

'Put me down,' she ordered. 'You don't know where I've been.'

Her copy of the opera fell on the pavement. 'Now look what you've done, Secombe. It's a good thing it is second-hand and not a new one.'

I picked it up and presented it with a bow.

'My apologies, Madam, I beg your pardon, Mademoiselle. My feelings got the better of me. I had been worried by your absence.'

'I shall remember that. You're an obvious case of "absence makes the heart grow fonder". See you in the playground after class.'

So saying she sprinted into the rehearsal leaving me a poor second in the race.

'The tenors sound a lot stronger,' commented Aneurin later, tongue in cheek. 'A distinct improvement since the break. Not to mention the change for the better in the soprano section.'

'It's a good thing Bertie Owen isn't here,' I whispered to my fellow tenor, Iorwerth. 'He'd claim the praise for himself.'

'I must say,' said Iorwerth, 'you are singing with a twenty decibel volume increase since the interval.'

'Would you like a lift home, Mr Secombe? I shall be passing your house,' enquired Eleanor as the singers began to leave in clusters of three or four.

'I'd be most grateful, Dr Davies. I shouldn't like to take you out of your way but if you are passing my digs, that is fine.'

Twenty minutes later when she had parked the car in a country lane, she said, 'You needn't sound so obsequious when I offer you a lift. It's so much out of character that it sounds suspicious.'

'Come here, Dr Davies,' I replied and smothered any further comment with a very enjoyable embrace for both participants.

'Would you let me get my breath back?' she murmured some time later. 'The reason for my lateness was a long talk I had with my parents.'

'I thought perhaps you had had a big bust up with them.'

'Now, look here, Frederick, it was not a big bust up. I simply

31

emphasised the fact that I had found someone to whom I would wish to be attached sooner rather than later and that nothing they could say would make any difference.'

'And the result?'

'The result was that they could see I was determined come hell or high water. All that they have asked is that we don't rush into anything this week or next. Furthermore, my dear, you have been invited to tea with the Davieses next Sunday afternoon.'

So saying, she kissed me lightly on the lips.

'You're an angel, a miracle worker. You really are,' I rhapsodised.

'Don't get carried away, Mr Secombe,' she replied, 'I'm not that good. Just be ready when I call for you on Sunday. Is half past three OK?'

'It will have to be a brief Sunday School in that case but I'm sure I can manage it, believe me.'

'I believe you. Now shall we go?'

Half an hour later she dropped me off at my digs. No sooner had I entered the house than Mrs Richards came out of the middle room, looking flustered.

'Don't take your coat off, Mr Secombe. A man's just come down with a message from the hospital. He said his name was Mr Porter and that Mrs Llewellyn told him to come here. Anyway there's a black baby been born, and it's in a tent in the ward and they want you to christen it straight away.'

I ran up the stairs two at a time, grabbed my cassock and surplice off the hook in my wardrobe and was out through the door in a flash. It was a steep climb to the hospital. By the time I reached the entrance, my heart was pounding and my lungs were bursting.

'This way, reverend,' said the porter. He led me up a flight of stairs to the maternity ward. My legs were beginning to buckle under me.

'You look all in,' said the sister after I had been ushered into her office. 'Sit down for a minute and get your breath back. Have you ever baptised a baby in an oxygen tent?'

'I'm afraid not,' I gasped.

'It's quite simple. I'll take the top off the tent and you squeeze a few drops of warm water from a piece of cotton wool on to the baby's forehead. By the way you needn't have brought your

32

robes with you. The old Vicar didn't dress up.'

'That's good enough for me,' I said. 'I shan't bother either.'

'Just bring your prayer book with you and come and meet the mother. It's her first baby and she's very distressed. Her husband's away in the forces, you see.'

Her mention of the prayer book made my heart stop. I had forgotten to bring it with me. The colour drained from my face.

'What's the matter, Reverend?' she asked. 'Are you feeling ill?'

'It's – it's the prayer book. I've forgotten to bring it.'

'Not to worry, my dear.' She was a grey-haired, motherly figure, short and plump. 'I'm sure you know the words of the baptism. You can make up a little prayer for the baby and his mother. As long as you say something she'll be only too pleased. By the way, the baby's to be christened David William.'

I followed her into a side ward occupied by sleeping babies in their cots. In the corner by the oxygen tent stood a teenage mother in a hospital dressing gown, dabbing her eyes with a handkerchief and staring down at her child.

'This is the clergyman, Mary,' said the sister gently. The girl raised her eyes to my face.

'I 'ope you can do something.' She spoke in a whisper.

'Let's hope God will,' I managed to say. The sister handed me a beaker half-full of warm water and a piece of cotton wool. Then she opened the top of the tent to reveal a tiny naked human being, his blue face contorted, with a tube inserted in his nose, his belly expanding and contracting every split second, it seemed.

With a shaking hand I dipped the ball of cotton wool into the beaker.

'David William,' I heard myself say, 'I baptise you in the name of the Father', I managed to get one small drop of water on the baby's forehead, 'and of the Son', another drop, 'and of the Holy Ghost. Amen.' I wasn't sure whether a third drop had followed. I knew God would understand if it had not. 'Let us pray,' I went on. 'Our Father . . .' The two women joined me in the Lord's Prayer. Then there was a silence while I collected my thoughts.

'If it be your will, O God,' I extemporised, 'let this child live and give strength to his mother in her time of trial for Jesus

Christ's sake. And the blessing of God Almighty, the Father, the Son and the Holy Ghost be with you both now and always. Amen.'

The sister replaced the cover on the tent as soon as I had finished. My clothes were sticking to my body and my legs were giving up their support.

'You'd better come back to my office and have a cup of tea,' suggested the sister.

'Thank you, Reverend,' said the baby's mother. 'I feel better now he's been done and you've said a little prayer.'

With the help of that vote of thanks and a strong cup of tea, I felt a different person when I left the sister's office.

I passed the porter on the way out.

'You've put the drops of water on the baby then,' he said. 'I don't know what good they think that do do.'

'It's not what they think, you think or I think that matters,' I snapped. 'It's what God thinks and I'm quite prepared to leave it to him.'

Before he could say anything else, I had descended the steps in a much more lively fashion than I had climbed them. The night air was cool and pleasant. Pontywen was asleep and I was wide awake, with a mission accomplished. Now it was up to God.

4

'How was that black baby?' enquired Mrs Richards at breakfast next morning.

'It wasn't black. It was blue,' I replied.

'Well, well!' she said. 'Fancy that. You do learn something every day. Blue babies. I wonder what other colours they'll be next. These scientists in their lavatories. They're getting too clever with that bomb in atoms and all that.'

I had slept fitfully. My mind refused to surrender totally to oblivion. Eleanor's face alternated with the tiny contorted features of David William in a series of images which included the occasional intrusion of a curlered Mrs Greenfield.

As soon as breakfast was over, I made my way to the hospital. The sun was shining low in the sky, just managing to climb over the pyramids of slag on the hilltop across the valley. Not a shred of cloud desecrated the blue expanse.

'God's in his heaven, all's right with the world,' I said to myself as I strolled leisurely up the hill, savouring the fresh air and the sunshine.

A few minutes later I was knocking on the door of the sister's office in the maternity ward.

'Come in,' barked a voice.

Seated at her desk was a stern-faced dyed-haired ogress in sister's uniform. My kind friend had gone off duty.

'I – er – baptised a baby, David William, in an oxygen tent late last night. I've come to see how he is.'

'It's a good thing you've come, Reverend. The baby died about an hour ago and the mother's distressed. You'll find her in the side ward opposite.'

She spoke in a tone as impersonal as that of a wireless

announcer reading the fat stock prices. My heart sank. I was convinced that the baby would recover and that I would be greeted by a happy and grateful mother.

'Thank you, Sister,' I said and closed the door. It was a minute or two before I could bring myself to knock on the door opposite.

I gave a gentle tap. There was no reply. I tapped again and opened the door a few inches.

'May I come in?' I asked.

'Oh it's you, Reverend. Come in, please.'

The young mother was seated on a chair by an empty bed. Her face was tear stained and her hands were grasped tight together.

She looked up.

'Why did He take him when He'd only just given him to me?'

Her voice was hoarse from too much weeping.

I took her hands into mine. Pious platitudes were not going to help. In any case, since I was near to tears myself, I could not have manufactured them.

'To be honest, Mary, I wish I knew.' I stood silent, holding her hands, incapable of any more words for the moment. The tension in her hands eased slightly, as she continued to stare at the floor.

'Shall we say the Lord's Prayer together?' I asked after a few minutes.

She nodded without raising her head.

I said a home-made prayer for little David William and for herself and then gave her the blessing.

Mary raised her head and looked me full in the face. 'Thank you,' she said. 'You have been a great help. Will you do me just one more favour?'

'If I can, I will,' I promised.

'Will you bury my baby?'

'Certainly I will.'

'I don't want no one else to do it.'

She began to weep quietly.

'Come on now,' I said. 'You have been very good.'

She dried her eyes.

'My husband's coming home on leave from the forces today. Compassionate leave. So that will brighten me up.'

As I made my way down the hill, dark clouds were beginning

to accumulate. 'Fine before seven, rain by eleven,' I told myself. I should have remembered that. It would have been a useful corrective to my earlier euphoria.

By the time I was turning the corner into Mount Pleasant View, the rain had begun to come down heavily. My heart sank when I saw Evan the Post advancing towards me. Tall, thin, white haired, the postman was a local character and a great talker who had buttonholed me on more than one occasion.

'Morning, Mr Secombe. Turned nasty again.' He stood blocking my path.

'You're from Swansea, aren't you?'

I nodded.

'I've just been thinking, it was a day like this many years ago, long before you were born, when Swansea were playing Newport at Rodney Parade. Swansea 'ad the finest 'arf-back who ever played for Wales – Billy Trew. Two minutes to go, Newport leading three points to nil, and in the Swansea 'arf. A line-out, ball comes to Billy Trew, kicked into touch in the Newport 'arf.'

The rain was trickling down the back of my neck, but there was no escape.

'Another line-out, back comes the ball to Billy Trew, kicked into touch just outside the Newport twenty-five. Another line-out, back comes the ball to Billy Trew, beats one man, then two. Then he kicks, perfect trajectory, goes through the posts, like slicing a lemon in 'arf. The final whistle goes. Newport three – Swansea four. But who did it all, Billy Trew.'

'Fantastic,' I said.

'I remember meeting one of the old internationals outside the Red Lion –'

I decided I had to get to my digs before being submerged in the downpour.

'Excuse me, Mr Phillips, but there's somebody waiting to see me in my lodgings.'

He stood aside reluctantly.

'Tell you some more about Billy Trew when you've got more time.'

'You do that, Mr Phillips. Good morning.'

I was up the steps and into number thirteen before he could look round.

My landlady met me in the hall.

'You look like a drowned cat, Mr Secombe. You'd better dry your hair quick after you've taken your coat off.'

'It's Evan the Post's fault. He pinned me to the pavement for five minutes in the pouring rain, telling me all about a rugby match donkey's years ago.'

'Oh, him! He do spend more time talking than walking. It's a wonder the letters ever get done. He's a real old appleman. Anyway, you've got a visitor in the front room, Idris the Milk.'

'So there was someone waiting to see me after all, and he couldn't be more welcome.'

She looked at me in bewilderment.

In a couple of minutes I had divested myself of my outer clothing, dried my hair and made myself presentable to meet my visitor.

Idris Shoemaker, son of a German emigrant named Schumacher, was our local milkman and a chorister at St Padarn's. Not only that, he was a friend at whose house on occasional evenings I was a guest for a fish and chip supper. His young son Percy was a choirboy and his four-year-old daughter Elsie was an impish cherub. Together with his tiny blue eyed wife Gwen, they formed a delightful family in whose presence a curate could relax, knowing that within the four walls of their living room anything said would go no further.

He was still wearing his milkman's apron and was seated in my armchair by the fire, his eyes heavy-lidded as if he had been asleep. Idris had a tendency to drop off once he sat down by a fireside.

'Who's been dozing off then?' I asked.

He struggled to his feet.

'Sorry, Mr Secombe. Come and sit in your chair by 'ere.'

'It's all right, Idris. Only joking. You sit there and rest your legs. You've been on them much longer than I have.'

I drew up a chair on the opposite side of the fireplace.

'What can I do for you?' I asked.

'Well, it's more of a case of what I can do for you,' he replied.

'That's interesting, Idris. Come on, out with it.'

''Ow would you like to come and see a show tonight and come back for fish and chips after?'

'I can't think of anything better. What show is this?' I asked.

'It's the Abergelly Amateur Operatic. They're doing *New Moon* – it's a new company started up. First show in the Valley since the war. It means a bus down there and the late bus back, mind.'

'I'd love to come. But what about Gwen, isn't she coming?'

'Looks like Elsie's got the measles. We've got two tickets and Gwen thought you'd like to come in 'er place.'

'That's very kind, Idris. I come on one condition that I pay for my ticket and I pay the bus fares.'

'We'll see about that later. Right then.' He struggled to his feet. 'It's best if we catch the ten-past six.'

'OK,' I said. 'I'll be down at your place at about quarter to six to see how Elsie's coping with her measles.'

'How's that little baby,' enquired Mrs Richards after Idris had gone.

'I'm afraid he's dead, but the mother is very brave about it. She's asked me to do the funeral next week.'

'That's what you get when you put those poor little things in tents. They're getting far too clever, it strikes me, interfering with mother's nature.'

By the time I set out for the Shoemaker abode that evening the rain had given way to dry crisp weather. A waning full moon vied with the few standard lamps in lighting the wet streets.

Elsie was ensconced in her father's armchair, wrapped in a blanket and looking very sorry for herself. She was not at all like a friend of mine when I was her age. I went to visit the invalid in his bedroom and found him riding a rocking horse. 'Come in, Fred,' he shouted. 'Isn't it great? I've got the bloody measles. No school.'

'She's stayed up until you've come, Mr Secombe,' said Gwen.

The little girl's eyes were swollen with the virus and her face was plastered with the rash. However, she managed a small grin.

I presented her with a bag of dolly mixtures, and kissed her cheek.

'Thank you very much,' she whispered.

'You shouldn't waste your sweet coupons like that,' her mother said.

'I don't call that waste,' I replied. 'I'm sure they're more welcome to her than they are to me.'

39

There was a long queue waiting at the bus stop and we had to stand all the way to Abergelly. It seemed that the whole bus load were on their way to the show. The bus disgorged its passengers outside the Miners' Welfare hall, the venue for the performance.

The excitement among the crowd milling around outside the hall was intense. Evidently the first musical to be performed in the valley since the war was eagerly anticipated.

'We've got good seats up in the balcony,' said Idris. 'Gwen and me always go up there if we can for any show.'

Elderly men in dinner suits which reeked of moth protection for the past five years directed the crowd up the stairs and into their seats. Elderly ladies in evening dresses with a similar redolence sold programmes. Culture had returned to the Valley.

The hubbub in the hall drowned the tuning up of the orchestra in the pit. It was obvious that sweet coupons had been squandered for the occasion as bags of sweets were transferred along the rows as quickly as a rugby ball in the three-quarter line at Cardiff Arms Park.

''Ave a liquorice all-sort?' said Idris, producing a bag from the pocket of his best suit.

'I don't know what this lot are like. They've only been formed since last May, I know they've got some from Pontywen in it. We'll 'ave to wait and see.'

'Looking at the programme, Idris,' I observed, 'the show seems to be a mighty tall order for a new society. The first scene in the Grand Salon of Monsieur Beauvoir's Mansion near New Orleans, with four scene changes to follow in the first act and with six scene changes in the second act. Add to that the fact that the action of the play is set in the years 1792–3 with a costume problem involved.'

'Well, I saw it done before the war over in Cwmberis and the society there did a good job. The first scene was marvellous. They had a balcony where the heroine made her entrance. There must have been a chorus of about forty or fifty, and they were great.'

Idris was annoyed that a Swansea Jack, as a native of my home town was nicknamed, should try to belittle what a valley society could do.

'In that case I shall look forward to the evening,' I said and popped a liquorice all-sort in my mouth to prevent it making any more remarks.

Soon the lights dimmed and the audience composed themselves. The musical director, Morgan Lloyd-Williams, took his place at the rostrum to enthusiastic applause and led his orchestra of fifteen players into the overture. Idris was right. It was a workman-like performance indeed. The well loved melodies from the musical whetted the appetite for what was to follow.

Then the curtains opened. Immediately it was apparent that this was a production much inferior to that of the Cwmberis society. There was no balcony, a few flats badly painted interspersed with curtains. The only resemblance to the pre-war production was the large number of ladies in the chorus, most of whom were obviously veteran performers, who were singing that they were young and fair maidens wanting to be kissed.

There followed the entrance of Viscount Ribaud, announced by the butler who bowed his head as his master appeared and as a result dropped his wig on the floor.

Even more disastrous was the entrance of Marianne, the heroine. Evidently it was intended that she should appear on the balcony in response to the men who were singing below, 'Marianne we want to love you'. A massive wall of maidens was blocking entrance upper stage right floor level, while the ten males were singing their hearts out stage left.

It seemed that Marianne was making a valiant effort to push her way throught the mêlée upper stage right. The orchestra had stopped and the musical director, baton upraised, awaited her appearance, shaking his head in despair. Eventually she appeared, a tall thin lady in her forties, visibly exhausted by her forcible entry and uncertain of the key in which her first unaccompanied notes were intended to be sung. The pianist sprang to her aid with a note she seemed reluctant to take. He repeated the note with the vigour of an enthusiastic piano tuner. She nodded her thanks and launched into her opening number which was drowned by the male chorus all singing bel canto.

By now I was finding great difficulty in controlling my mirth. Idris was staring grimly at the stage, as if he were watching Wales slide into an ignominious defeat.

A little later, Robert the hero, a short fat baritone, with a beer belly emphasized by a bare-chested outfit he was wearing,

41

led on two men who were supposed to be bearing trunks on their shoulders. Instead they carried large suitcases which looked as if they had been purchased recently at Marks & Spencer.

Then came a scene in which Robert was heard singing off stage. Viscount Ribaud said, 'He's a desperate criminal. I'll take no chance. There he is with a ray of moonlight on him, a perfect target.' He took his pistol and pressed the trigger – the gun failed to go off. He levelled the weapon and fired again to no avail – once more he raised the gun. By this time the musical director decided to intervene. He nodded to the drummer who gave his tympanum a hearty whack on the side, only to find that the pistol did go off, giving the impression of a nasty ricochet.

'Bloody 'ell!' exploded Idris. 'Sorry, Mr Secombe.'

'Don't apologise,' I said. 'I'm sure your other societies are better than this. Perhaps it will improve in the second act.'

It did not.

Half-way through Act 2 in Scene 3, 'The Stockade one year later', one of the flats collapsed, revealing three surprised men, in bracered trousers holding three half-full beer mugs in their hands. As the cast made frantic efforts to push the flat back up the curtains came across quickly to hide their embarrassment.

However the climax came in the finale of Act 2, Scene 5, 'Marianne's Cabin later that evening'. Throughout the performance, the hero, Robert, had given the impression that he was a traffic policeman on duty at a busy road junction in Cardiff. Every manufactured gesture was accompanied by a completely emotionless face.

'One kiss, one girl to save it for,' sang the hero of five foot six, standing some distance away from his heroine of five foot eight. 'All my life, I'll love only one girl and no other girl in the world.' He moved further away from his beloved. This was too much for the musical director.

'For God's sake, kiss her,' he said in a stage whisper which was audible at the back of the hall.

The baritone advanced upon the heroine, gave her a peck on the cheek and then retreated a yard from her.

I had been using my handkerchief extensively as the performance was winding its way to its end. After I arrived home, I found I had bitten it through when the peck on the cheek occurred.

As the audience filed out of the hall, the mood was subdued and more appropriate to the aftermath of a funeral.

'Sorry you had to sit through that,' mumbled Idris.

'Don't worry,' I said. 'There were some things I enjoyed immensely.'

'Such as?'

'The orchestra was very good and the chorus sang quite well. Even all those slip ups were amusing.'

'I'm glad you think so. You'll 'ear and see a lot better than that next year.'

'Yes, Idris. In St Padarn's Church Gilbert and Sullivan Society's production of *The Pirates of Penzance* for a start. What about you joining us? You've got a good bass voice. You'd make a great Sergeant of Police.'

We were waiting at the bus stop for the last bus back to Pontywen, emitting clouds of frosty breath into sharp night air. My suggestion caused him to puff out a plethora of clouds, as he pondered over his reply.

He pondered all the way back to Pontywen. It was not until we were in Evans' chip shop that he gave me his decision, against a background of beery singing and banter provided by fugitives from the Workingmen's Club.

'I wouldn't mind 'aving a go. If you thought I was any good, OK. If not, you'd 'ave to tell me. I've never done any acting except in the Church Passion plays years ago.'

'Done,' I said, and we shook hands on the deal.

'Just met, 'ave you?' asked a drunk behind us in the queue.

When we arrived at Idris' house, the plates were warming in the hearth in front of a blazing fire in the grate. The table was laid and five minutes later we were tucking into Evans' fish and chips, best in the valley, according to Idris.

'Mr Secombe 'as asked me to join 'is society,' said Idris to Gwen whose eyes were heavy-lidded until then. Now they opened wide.

'He's no Ronald Colman,' she replied. 'I know he can sing a bit but as for acting or anything – well.'

'I'm positive he'll make a good Sergeant of Police in *The Pirates of Penzance*,' I said. 'Anyway, we'll see. At least he said he's willing to have a go.'

'That's up to him. What was *The New Moon* like?' she asked.

'Terrible,' pronounced Idris.

'Well, I had my money's worth,' I said and put a ten shilling note on the table, part of the proceeds from the lady bookmaker's gift.

Before there could be any attempt to push the note back into my pocket, I dashed into the hall, picked up my overcoat and opened the door.

'Thanks for a nice evening,' I shouted and strode up the street to Mount Pleasant View.

When I arrived at my digs, I found a note on my table. It was from my inept colleague, Charles Wentworth-Baxter.

'I think I've got laryngitis. Can you get somebody for St Padarn's tomorrow morning? Charles.'

5

I had a sleepless night. At two o'clock in the morning, I came downstairs and made myself a cup of tea, all the time harbouring murderous thoughts about my colleague. My first Sunday of sole charge was off to a disastrous start. I wondered if that were a bad omen for my rendezvous with Eleanor's parents later in the day.

By seven o'clock I was washed and dressed, ready to go to the Vicarage and phone the Rural Dean. On further reflection I decided against it. The old man would not have come to his senses until nine at the earliest and the service at St Padarn's was due to begin at nine-thirty. Not only that, I was due at the parish church to take the Communion service at eight. Something had to be done before then.

At half-past seven I was hammering on the back door of Moelwyn Howells' greengrocers' shop. A few minutes later, a dishevelled figure in shirt and trousers appeared, bleary eyed and bewildered.

'You're up early,' croaked Moelwyn. 'Can't you sleep?'

'You've hit the nail on the head,' I said. 'It's your lodger. He left a note last night for me saying he had laryngitis and couldn't take the service at St Padarn's.'

'I don't know anything about it, as God is my judge,' replied the greengrocer.

'In that case, do you mind if I go up to his bedroom and have words with him?'

'Be my guest,' said Moelwyn. 'You know which room it is.'

I ran up the stairs two at a time and banged on Charles's door before throwing it open like a detective on a police raid.

He sat bolt upright in his bed, open mouthed and staring at the intruder.

'Fred!' he shouted. 'What's the matter?'

'For someone suffering from laryngitis, you've made a quick recovery,' I snarled. 'Come off it, Charles. You get down to St Padarn's for the half-past nine. If your voice goes, use semaphore.'

He was still staring as I closed the door and went downstairs.

Moelwyn was standing at the foot of the stairs. 'I'm sorry about all this but see that he gets up in time to take the service, please,' I said.

'Don't worry, Mr Secombe, I will.' It was obvious by the look on his face that he would ensure that the Reverend Charles Wentworth-Baxter would be at the altar for the Holy Communion Service.

As I made my way to the parish church I felt that the late Vicar of Pontywen would have been proud of me.

Bertie Owen met me at the door of St Padarn's when I arrived for Sunday School at half-past two. I could tell by his excited demeanour that he had news to impart about the morning service.

'Come on, Bertie, out with it. What has he done?' I demanded.

'Well, first of all, he was late getting here. We were all wondering if he was coming at all. Then he couldn't remember the prayer to say in the vestry with the choir. So he mumbled something like "one, two, three, four, Amen". Anyway that's what Idris the Milk thought.'

'A good start,' I said.

'You've heard nothing yet,' he went on. 'When he got up in the pulpit, he pulled out the sermon from his cassock pocket and found it was the one he preached last time he was here. "If you don't mind, I've got to read you the sermon you had at your harvest." You could hear the congregation groan, honest. It went on and on. When it came to getting the wine ready for the Communion, he knocked the chalice over. There was wine everywhere. Then at the end of giving out the bread and the wine, he didn't notice that Mrs Williams, Top shop and me were at the other end waiting to have ours. I had to go up to the altar and tap him on the shoulder. It was a real picnic, I can tell you.'

'Heaven preserve him when the new Vicar comes,' I said.

'Especially if it's that one I caught hold of at the Vicarage,' Bertie added.

'In that case it will be heaven preserve you both.'

The next hour dragged by in Sunday School as I waited for half-past three to come and Eleanor to arrive for my tea date with her parents. I was dressed in my Burton's best and as apprehensive as Charles must have felt earlier about his solo debut.

It was a truncated session for the children and their teachers. By twenty-five past three they had all gone, including Bertie who wanted to linger.

'You go. I'll lock up,' I said firmly.

He got the message and left forthwith.

Prompt at half-past three, Eleanor arrived.

'You're looking smart,' she commented. 'You've even combed your hair nicely. Must be going somewhere special.'

'Thanks for the backhanded compliment, but, I must say, it has done my morale a power of good. It needed a boost.'

'Now see here, Secombe.' She stopped the car and switched off the engine. 'Before we go any further I don't want any more defeatism from you. You are coming to tea with my parents, not going to an appointment with a firing squad.'

'Pax,' I said and settled back in my seat.

Some ten miles and fifteen minutes later we were entering the drive leading to the Davies residence, a large black and white Mock Tudor detached house overlooking an immaculate lawn bordered by shrubs and cypress trees. My inferiority complex ballooned, as I compared this building to the modest council house in which I had been brought up.

'For heaven's sake, don't look so scared,' said Eleanor.

My mouth had dried up and my top lip clove to my gums turning me into a Humphrey Bogart look alike.

'Remember,' she went on, 'that I love you and I want my parents to love you as well.' She squeezed my hand and then opened the car door.

It was with difficulty that my legs transported my body into the entrance hall. As I closed the front door, Eleanor announced our arrival in ringing tones. 'Hello, everybody, we're here!' A dog barked and a door opened.

A petite grey haired replica of Eleanor emerged, her clear blue eyes doing a survey of her daughter's intended. I made a short prayer for the seal of approval. It seemed to work because she smiled and advanced towards me, her hand outstretched. As she took my hand, I could see that the smile was more in her mouth than her eyes. Some more prayer would be needed, evidently.

'Mummy, this is Fred,' came the introduction.

'How do you do, Mr Secombe?' said Mrs Davies in tepid tones.

'His name is Fred.' Eleanor's temper was beginning to rise.

'I am only trying to be polite, Eleanor,' snapped her mother.

It was evident that a fraught tea time lay ahead. My top lip was now reunited with my gum in a permanent embrace, it seemed.

'Where's Daddy, anyway?' asked my fuming beloved.

'He's only gone down to the village to post some letters. He's due back any time. Would you like to come into the sitting room, Mr Secombe?'

It was a spacious room, with french windows opening on to the lawn. An expensive three-piece suite reposed on a large expensive carpet. Two Buck prints of obscure Welsh castles adorned the walls, together with some watercolours of seascapes.

Eleanor took my hand in a fierce grip and led me to the three-seater where we sat side by side. Mrs Davies stood by the window. I waited for the interrogation to begin.

'Is this your first parish, Mr Secombe?'

'No, my second. I was a curate in a parish in Swansea before I came here. It was a working-class district, friendly people but I was unhappy with the training I was getting there. That is why I came to Pontywen – to get the benefit of serving under Canon Llewellyn. It was most unfortunate that my time with him was cut short so abruptly.'

'That was very sad, wasn't it? Do you come from a Vicarage background?'

'Not at all, my father is a commercial traveller for a wholesale grocery firm in Swansea. That's my home town and I'm proud of it.'

'In that case, it was a pity you had to leave it, wasn't it?'

'That's enough of the third degree, Mummy,' said Eleanor.

'Would you like a sherry, Fred?'

'I would, indeed, please.'

'Here's your father coming. You'd better pour him one as well. I don't think I'll have one for the moment.' So saying Mrs Davies went out of the room to greet her husband. I could hear a *sotto voce* conversation in the hall. My heart was pounding.

'Keep your end up, Secombe,' whispered Eleanor. 'You're as good as they are, if not better.'

It was the cue for the entry of her father. He was a man of medium height, bespectacled, grey moustached and of a sallow complexion. His brown tweed suit provided the country gentleman image – an image ill suited to his physical appearance.

'Daddy, this is Fred,' came introduction number two.

I stood up and collided with a coffee table on my way to shake his hand.

'Don't knock the furniture about, lad,' he said and shook my hand warmly. 'So you are Fred. We've heard a lot about you.'

'Thank God for daddy,' was the fervent prayer I sent up.

From that moment I began to relax, to the great relief of my top lip. When Eleanor disappeared into the kitchen to help her mother, we talked rugby as we sipped our sherry. The Davies residence began to assume the form of a home instead of an inquisitorial vault.

Then we went into the dining room for tea which was laid out on a refectory table. Dominating the cakes and sandwiches were sticks of celery. My heart sank. The last time I had seen a similar array on a refectory table was at the Bishop's Palace during the retreat before my ordination.

As a discipline the ordinands had to keep silence. It is not easy to eat celery under such circumstances. There were five of us at the table, at the head of which sat the Bishop. Four of us were munching sandwiches quietly and gazing intently at our plates when Charlie Williams bit into his celery. The crack echoed around the dining room. Charlie retained the large piece in his mouth for some time, hoping it would dissolve. As it showed no sign of doing so, he was forced to chew. He attempted a quick swallow to avoid further desecration of the silence and was in imminent danger of choking. He made a speedy escape from the room, knocking over his chair in the process.

By now the four of us were in serious danger of exploding.

The Bishop appeared to be unperturbed, thinking, no doubt, of the address he was to deliver later that evening. It was Arthur Morris who next decided on the kamikaze exploit. He played with the stick for some time, dipping it in the salt on his plate and staring at it as if he could mesmerise it into silent consumption. Then he bit the thing. It was a louder crack than Charlie Williams' effort. He did not stay to swallow but arose from the table and left in dignified fashion, with a mouthful of celery and a slight bow to the bishop who continued to stare into space.

This left three of us staring at our plates and fighting to suppress our unseemly mirth. The stock of sandwiches had dwindled to three – one apiece. As we munched our way through the remainder, the Bishop turned his attention on us. He coughed and with a wave of his hand indicated that there were still six sticks of celery waiting to be consumed. We looked at each other with a wild surmise, silent, on the peak of a dilemma. Then, providing a supreme example of ESP we rose as one man, gently shook our heads, bowed to the dignitary and fell over each other in a rapid exit. My ribs were still aching next morning from the laughter that followed when we reached the sanctuary of our dormitory.

Once more I was faced with the challenge of celery on a refectory table. I need not have worried. Eleanor and her father bit into the sticks with gusto, much to the annoyance of Mrs Davies whose glances towards them were positively hostile. Emboldened by the sherry and their example, I proceeded to bite into the celery in similar manner. Eleanor's mother discovered that there was a need for more hot water and departed into the kitchen. By the time she returned some minutes later, the celery had disappeared.

'Mummy doesn't like celery,' Eleanor explained.

'I don't like the taste and I can't stand the noise involved,' said her mother testily.

Half an hour later, Eleanor was driving me back to Pontywen in time for evensong. We stopped outside my digs in good time for the service. 'I like your father,' I said.

'But you don't like my mother.'

'I didn't say that.'

'Anyway, you implied it. I can't blame you. She didn't exactly make you feel welcome. In time, she will come to accept you. It's just that she wants the best for her daughter. That's why I say in time she will accept you, once she knows you better.'

She kissed me lightly on the lips and in no time the Morris Minor was chugging its way out of Mount Pleasant View.

'How did you get on?' enquired Mrs Richards.

'I found Dr Davies easy to get on with, but Mrs Davies was a different proposition,' I replied.

'She wasn't everybody's pot of tea when they were here in Pontywen,' said my landlady. 'Too toity hoity. Came from a high-class family in Cardiff. I think her father was a banister in the police courts.'

The congregation and choir at St Padarn's were still recovering from the Charles Wentworth-Baxter show at the Communion service that morning. Mrs Collier, leading soprano and wife of the organist, pounced on me as I entered the church. She had taken home the altar cloth to wash after its drenching in Communion wine.

'I've got it boiling in the copper but I don't know if it will get all that stain out,' she said.

'Don't worry. I'm sure it will all come out in the wash,' I assured her.

'Then we had the usual mix up with the hymn numbers,' she went on. 'My husband had to shout from the organ stool to correct him three times in the service.'

'At least you won't have that trouble this evening. It is the parish church organist who will have to suffer instead, not to mention the congregation.' So saying I made a beeline for the vestry where Bertie Owen was giving a graphic account of the morning's proceedings to those members of the choir who were fortunate enough to be absent. My colleague was making a name for himself in Pontywen. Soon he would be a legend in his own lifetime.

When I returned to my digs, to my surprise I found Mrs Llewellyn there. My first thought was that Charles had done something really outrageous at the parish church.

'I thought I had better let you know that I am leaving the Vicarage at the end of the week,' she said. 'My cousin has offered me accommodation until I can find some small place to live in.

Bournemouth will be heaven after Pontywen. I'm putting the furniture into storage.'

'It's a good thing you have your cousin to go to,' I replied. 'Staying on here for a few more months would be a lonely existence amongst all the memories you must have.'

'That's very true and it doesn't help when you have to put up with that young idiot in church. Evensong was a shambles. The only good thing was the shortness of his sermon. It must have been five minutes long at most. That's why I am here before you.'

'Would you like a cup of tea, Mrs Llewellyn?' I decided to ignore the reference to Charles. He had become more monotonous a topic than the weather.

'No thank you, Mr Secombe. I must get back and make a start with clearing up everything. By the way, I hear that the Board is meeting tomorrow to appoint the new vicar. If that man Whittaker is selected, I don't think Mr Wentworth-Baxter will be in Pontywen much longer.'

'We'll have to wait and see,' I said.

It was not a long wait. By Tuesday morning Father John Whittaker was knocking on my door, his appearance completely changed since his last foray into Pontywen. He was clad all in black, black raincoat, black suit and topping the outfit, a black ten gallon hat. With his five-foot-five stature and his hornrimmed spectacles, he looked like a comic advertisement for Sandeman's port.

'After my last experience', he intoned, 'I thought I had better come here rather than to the Vicarage.'

I ushered him into my room. He divested himself of his raincoat and hat and plunged himself into my armchair.

'This morning,' he went on, 'I received a letter from the Patronage Board offering me the living of Pontywen.' He delivered this information as if he were the mayor announcing the winner of a Parliamentary election on the steps of the Guildhall.

'Congratulations,' I said half-heartedly.

'I don't know whether it is cause for congratulations or not, until I have surveyed the land, as it were. When you follow an incumbent who has been in a parish as long as the late Canon Llewellyn, it is no easy task. However, I thrive on a challenge and I shall accept the nomination to the living.'

He paused and waited for further acclaim for his courage in facing the 'no easy task'. I found I was unable to massage his ego. Words would have stuck in my throat. Obviously disappointed by my silence, he became petulant.

'By the way, I don't want any changes in the status quo of services and so on during the interregnum. The changes will come when I arrive and not before.'

'I have no intention of changing anything, Vicar. The Bishop has put me in charge of operations until you arrive and I am answerable to him in the interim period.'

'Well, I can tell you that the interim period will not be long. I understand that Mrs Llewellyn is vacating the Vicarage by the end of the week. It means that next week I can make a list of what needs doing in the house. I hope to be inducted in a couple of months' time. Now is there anything you want to tell me about the parish?'

'As far as I am concerned, the parish is in good heart. Canon Llewellyn was a fine priest. He has left you a complete index of all church people in Pontywen, with his own comments on each card.'

'One of my first actions will be to inaugurate a survey of the *whole* of the parish – every house. I want a complete picture of its population. Is there anything else I should know?'

'There is one thing, some weeks ago I formed a Gilbert and Sullivan Society at St Padarn's and we have begun music rehearsals for a production of *The Pirates of Penzance*. I had full permission from the late Vicar.'

He stared at me in disbelief.

'Canon Llewellyn gave you permission for that?'

'He did indeed.'

'In that case, I can't very well withdraw that, but, I tell you this, if I had been here you wouldn't have got it. It's not a parish priest's job to run secular activities. Our concern is for souls not soloists.'

He liked that last sentence, so much so that he repeated the words 'souls not soloists'. I had an urgent desire to vomit.

He stood up.

'Now then,' he said. 'I'd like to visit the three churches. The car's outside. Before I do that, I wonder if I might wash my hands.'

The first occasion on which I had heard that euphemism was when as a student I was visited at my council house home by the Bishop's Chaplain. My mother had gone out for the afternoon and I had just emptied the teapot into the sink prior to preparing a pot of tea for my visitor.

A knock at the door interrupted my preparations. It was the Chaplain.

'Before I do anything else,' he said, 'I must wash my hands.'

Somewhat puzzled by the request I led him to the sink which was half full of tea leaves.

'I'll get you a towel. The soap is there at the side.'

'It's not a towel I want. It's a visit to your lavatory.' By this time, he was almost crossing his legs. I leapt up the stairs two at a time and led him to the haven where he would be. He refused the offer of a cup of tea. I think the sight of the tea leaves had turned his stomach.

While Father John Whittaker was 'washing his hands' in the outside lavatory, I looked out of the window at his car. It was an Austin Big Seven, in good condition and positively gleaming, not like Canon Llewellyn's old Morris. 'The old order changeth,' I said to myself.

Suddenly Charles Wentworth-Baxter appeared outside, looking very excited. He ran up the steps and banged on the door.

As I left my room to let him in, the Vicar designate came into the hall. I opened the door to my colleague.

'Have you heard the news? That awful Father bloke has been offered the living,' he announced.

'Charles,' I said quickly, 'this is Father Whittaker. He has come to look round the parish.'

The colour left my fellow curate's face and a sickly smile appeared.

It was a chilly atmosphere in the Austin Big Seven as we made a tour of the three churches.

'I'll be in touch,' promised our Vicar to be. It sounded more like a threat than a promise.

6

Later that day at half-past two, Full-Back Jones and I were standing at the churchyard gate waiting for Mr Matthews the undertaker to appear with the parents of David William and the body of their three-day-old son. It was a raw November afternoon, with a cold north-westerly wind blowing down the valley.

'Typical of 'im,' grumbled the gravedigger. 'Quarter-past two it was supposed to be.'

'It may not be Mr Matthews' fault. Perhaps the parents weren't ready,' I replied. 'All I know is that it is getting very chilly.'

''Ave a drop of this,' he said, producing a whisky flask from the filthy old raincoat which permanently adorned him.

'No thank you. I never drink the stuff and I don't want to breathe the smell of it over the bereaved, in any case.'

He put the flask back into his coat, looking aggrieved that his kind offer had been spurned.

A couple of minutes later an ancient black limousine pulled up outside. Full-Back Jones retreated to the little grave he had dug near the yew tree adjacent to the churchyard. 'Well, we always bring 'em 'ere,' he had said when I requested his services.

Mr Matthews left his front seat to open the door for Mary and her husband. They both wore black armbands over their overcoats. Mary's husband had his arm tightly round her shoulders. She was pale but tearless. The undertaker returned to the front seat and produced a pathetically small wooden box wrapped in white calico, with a name plate attached. Inside were the mortal remains of David William.

I led the procession to the grave, Mr Matthews following

behind me, holding the box, with Mary and her husband bringing up the rear. "'Man that is born of a woman hath but a short time to live,'" I intoned. Just three days, I said to myself. "'The Lord gave and the Lord hath taken away.'" Why, oh, why?

When we reached the graveside, the words of the Book of Common Prayer were not appropriate to the burial of a baby. 'Deliver us not into the bitter pains of eternal death.' Instead I spoke the words of Jesus when his disciples were turning away children from his presence.

'Suffer the little children to come unto me.' This was the one crumb of comfort I could offer to the parents. I prayed for them in their grief. We said the Lord's Prayer together.

Full-Back Jones took the box from the undertaker very reverently and placed it in the small hole he had dug. I committed the child into the loving arms of his Maker and the ceremony was over.

Mary and her husband stood silently for a minute or so, with their arms round each other. Then they turned away. She was still tearless. The previous days had drained her of every drop.

'This is Iorwerth, my husband.'

He was a tall young man. Evidently his army training had developed his physique greatly since his civilian days. His overcoat seemed several sizes too small for him. He shook my hand warmly.

'Thank you very much for all you've done. Mary says you've been a great help.'

'It's very kind of you to say so. I wish I could have helped more than I have done.'

'All I can say,' replied Mary, 'is that you couldn't have done more.'

They went off, hand in hand, following Mr Matthews who had made a beeline for the car. The gravedigger shovelled a few spades full of earth to cover the hole in the ground and David William disappeared, never to be seen again after his brief sojourn in this world.

After the funeral I went across to the Vicarage which adjoined the churchyard. There I found Mrs Llewellyn packing her belongings in a tea chest.

'I take it that you have heard the name of the next Vicar,' I said to her. 'Everybody else seems to have.'

'The Rural Dean rang me up this morning with the bad news. I don't think he's very happy about the appointment, either. Still it's only what I expected. Thank heavens I'm going.' The widow sounded almost happy.

'By the way,' she went on, 'the Rural Dean said that he's coming round to see you tomorrow afternoon.'

He arrived as Mrs Richards and I were halfway through our midday meal. I knew a minister in my previous parish who used to make a habit of doing that. It was said that the only meal he had at home was his Sunday dinner. However, it was immediately apparent that the old man was not interested in free food.

'Very sorry to interrupt your dinner, Mr Sembone.' Invariably he had great difficulty in remembering my name. 'My wife has gone shopping and visiting a friend. I've got to meet her by the clock in the square by half-past two. You carry on with your eating. I'll wait here and read your newspaper till you've finished.'

Mrs Richards was scathing when I returned to the middle room for the remainder of the meal.

'He may be the Rural Dean, but you think he would have been more considering. Does he think the world has got to stand still for his inconvenience?'

When I returned to my room, I found him asleep under my copy of *The Times*, deep in my armchair. He awoke with a start.

'Ah, Mr Seabourne, you've finished your dinner then and I've just finished reading your paper, so that's fine, isn't it? Well, now, the reason for my calling is – er – how shall I put it?' He paused, pink with embarrassment.

'I don't want to interfere,' he went on, studying the ceiling. 'You know I'm not like that. But – what it is, is this.' He cleared his throat. 'It's these old farmers up at Llanhyfryd. They're so tight-fisted.'

'Don't go on any further, Mr Rural Dean, I know what you're going to say. They object to paying for a taxi to bring the lay reader for Sunday service.'

'Well, well. You've hit the nail on the head straight away.'

'I had no alternative, I'm afraid. Ezekiel Evans has no car and can't ride a bicycle. It's a bit much to expect him to walk four miles there and four miles back.'

'Quite right indeed. But what Mr Jones Blaenycwm Farm suggested was that you or your colleague could walk it quite easily, being young men.'

Mr Jones, Blaenycwm Farm, was the Vicar's Warden, a man whose flocks and whose herds had multiplied unlike the size of his generosity. My hackles rose.

'With all the money he's got tucked away, he could afford to buy a car to bring the preacher,' I exploded.

'Now, now. Calm down, Mr Surcombe. I'm only saying what he told me over the telephone.' The old man arose from my armchair. 'I've passed on the message. So I'll be off now.' The quickness of his exit belied his age.

I was so incensed by the meanness of Jones, Blaenycwm, that I decided to walk there that afternoon and confront him. It was a grey, cold day, in tune with the greyness of Pontywen. I hurried my steps, both to increase my body warmth and also to expedite my escape from the grim surroundings.

Once I was out into the countryside, the green vista began to soften my anger. The smells of industry evaporated and the fresh smell of rain-soaked hedges scented the air. Four miles later as the farm gates of Blaenycwm appeared, I commended myself on my initiative. A splendid walk and now I would administer a *coup de grâce* on Mr Evan Jones.

The farm road snaked its way to the Jones residence and farm buildings. It was more like a primitive cart track than a road. As I walked, I recalled my first visit to the countryside with my parents when we stayed with my father's cousins who had a smallholding in Cardiganshire. Coming from the docks district in Swansea, the world of agriculture was alien to me as a child.

When I was taken to see the cows milked in the smelly cowshed, I was appalled. 'We don't have our milk from those dirty old animals,' I said. 'We have ours in nice clean bottles.'

Another memory came to my mind. It was of my father returning to the farmhouse with blood streaming from his cheek and with a large tear in his trousers. He fancied himself as something of a marksman and had borrowed a shotgun to go rabbit shooting.

On his safari travels he had climbed over a barbed wire fence to stalk his prey. What he had not realised was that in the field there was a bull about to stalk his human prey. Some seconds later he heard the sound of hoofs and turned to see the animal coming towards him. My father ran for his life, climbed up the hedge near a tree, caught his trousers in the barbed wire and pierced his cheek with the sharp end of a branch. He ended up with stitches in his cheek, stitches in his trousers and the sharp end of my mother's tongue.

It was a steep climb to Blaenycwm Farmhouse. I paused near the top of the road to regain my breath and to admire the view of the distant mountains. Suddenly I was aware of a presence behind me. The next second there was a growl and teeth bit into the calf of my leg. It was a black and white farm dog, snarling and about to attack me again. I wished I were my father with his shotgun.

All I had was my one good leg, my left one. That was fortunate for me since I was left footed. I packed quite a punch in my left foot when I played soccer. The dog discovered that as my boot connected with his ribs. A piercing yelp rent the air asunder and the creature beat a rapid retreat in the direction of the farmhouse.

I rolled up my trouser leg to examine the damage to my limb. The hound had bitten through the skin and blood was oozing from the teeth marks. As I stood, contemplating the onset of tetanus or hydrophobia or both, there was an angry shout.

'W-what have you d-done to the d-dog?'

Coming towards me was the diminutive figure of Evan Jones, a rosy cheeked, grey haired man, clad in ancient tweed trousers and moth eaten pullover, and filthy wellingtons.

'You had better come and see what the dog has done to me,' I said indignantly, standing with my rolled trouser leg like a novitiate into the order of Freemasonry.

The length of the farmer's stride diminished and the purple flush of indignation vanished.

'B-bitten you, has he?' There was no solicitude in his voice.

'I'm afraid so, Mr Jones.'

He examined the injury for a second.

'He's only just b-broken the s-skin. That's n-nothing.'

'It may be nothing to you, Mr Jones, but it could mean tetanus or something like that to me.'

He snorted his derision.

'That's a c-clean dog that is.'

'How can it be a clean dog when it has been around your farmyard all day? I shall have to get a tetanus injection from the doctor.'

'You d-do what you l-like, but it'll be a w-waste of the d-doctor's t-time. I'm s-sorry you've been b-bitten but there it is.'

My cup of wrath overflowed.

'Mr Jones. I came here this afternoon to inform you that under no circumstances would the Reverend Charles Wentworth-Baxter and myself walk to Llanhyfryd and back to take a service. It is now doubly certain that this will be the case. St Paul may have fought with wild beasts at Ephesus but neither I nor my colleague will risk any such encounter on the road to Llanhyfryd. Until the new Vicar arrives, a taxi will bring the person responsible for the service.'

So saying I unrolled the trouser leg and limped my way down the cart-track, leaving the little man speechless outside his farmyard.

As I walked, so the calf of my right leg began to pain me. Visions of an amputation became more vivid with each step that I took. I remembered a former student at college who died the day after an angling expedition when a cut in his hand was infected by contact with a rat's droppings on a river bank.

It was with great relief that I noticed a telephone box in the distance. I decided to phone my doctor sweetheart for reassurance. My heart sank when her mother answered my call.

'She has only just come in and is having a late lunch,' said Mrs Davies frostily, 'so don't keep her long.'

When Eleanor came on the line, I explained my predicament as tersely as I could.

'Stay where you are,' she ordered. 'I'll do a quick swallow of my meal to please my mother and if you'll excuse a doctor's indigestion I shall be with you in a quarter of an hour's time.'

That quarter of an hour dragged by until the old Moris Minor pulled up outside the telephone box.

'Secombe,' she said, 'if ever there was a man born to trouble it's you. First it was your buttocks now it's your calf.'

I first met Eleanor when I visited the doctor's surgery for treatment to my posterior which had adhered to the bath. Mrs Richards had given it a flick of paint, as she put it.

'Let's have a look at your injury. You needn't lower your trousers this time, just hoist your trouser leg.'

She showed a great deal more solicitude than the skinflint farmer.

'Nasty,' she pronounced. 'I'll take you to the surgery to get it cleaned up and I'll give you a tetanus jab just in case.'

'What about hydrophobia?' I asked.

'The dog wasn't frothing at the mouth, was it?'

'Not that I noticed.'

'Well, in that case, you needn't worry. I expect the postman must have had a few nips in his time from a hound like that. You won't die, my love, and you won't need an amputation. Never fear, Eleanor's here.'

With my leg bathed and bandaged and with an injection in my arm, I sat on the examination couch and recounted the Blaenycwm saga.

'Why don't you have a word with the Bishop?' suggested Eleanor. 'You can phone him now from here.'

'He may not be in,' I said. 'He's probably chairing one of those dreadful committees.'

'Look, Secombe. You won't lose anything by giving him a ring. If he's out, he's out. You can try again later.'

She led me to the telephone, found the number, rang it and then seconds later said 'Good afternoon, my lord, the Reverend Fred Secombe would like a word with you.'

I picked up the phone while she stood grinning at me.

'Good afternoon, my lord,' I said breathily. 'I wondered if I might have a word about a problem which has arisen over Llanhyfryd.'

'What kind of problem?' The Bishop sounded unusually testy.

'It's about transport to the church from Pontywen for those conducting the service. None of us have any means of getting there, except by hiring a car and the churchwarden at Llanhyfryd has objected to paying for it.'

'They don't have to pay for it,' said the Bishop. 'The money for that comes out of the sequestration fund. That's the sum which accrues to the incoming incumbent during the vacancy. All the wedding and funeral fees in the parish go to him. Any necessary expenses have to be deducted from that sum. So you can tell the churchwardens at Llanhyfryd that they will not have to pay for the car hire. They will be reimbursed. The Rural Dean should have told you that.'

'I'm afraid he did not, my lord. However, I know now. Thank you very much for your help.'

'Not at all, Mr Secombe. I'm sorry if I sounded a little short with you at the beginning. I've had two long committee meetings with much bigger problems to contend with than yours. By the way, I didn't know the parish had a secretary.'

'The lady's not a secretary. Just a friend who allowed me to use her phone.'

Eleanor held her hand over her mouth to suppress her laughter.

'Everything else in order? You know who your new Vicar is by now, I'm sure,' said the Bishop.

'Yes, my lord, he has been to visit all three churches. There aren't any other problems. Everything is going well.'

When I put down the phone, Eleanor burst into peals of laughter.

'The lady's not a secretary, just a friend,' she mimicked. 'That will raise the Bishop's eyebrows. A friend, eh?'

'I tell you what, my dear,' I said, 'you'll make a perfect Vicar's wife.'

'And I tell you what,' she replied, 'you'll make a perfect doctor's husband. You know so little about medicine that I can blind you with science anytime.'

'As to the object of my phone call,' I went on, 'you will be pleased to know that we can hire a car for the service at Llanhyfryd. Since the money for it will come out of money accruing to the new Vicar from fees, et cetera, I propose we hire a Rolls-Royce for each service.'

'You're a devious curate but I love you,' she said, giving me a peck on the cheek. 'Now, I'd better get back home, otherwise I shall be in trouble. I'll drop you off on the way. You'd better put your leg up for the rest of the evening. Doctor's orders.'

Mrs Richards was disgusted at Evan Jones' attitude to the dog bite.

'Fancy saying that it was nothing to worry about. You could have had all kinds of inflections from that dirty old dog. Anyway you go and sit in the front room. I've got something special for your tea, devilish kidneys. I'll bring them in on a tray. My husband used to like that. It's the first time I've had them from the butcher since the war.'

I had no sooner put the first forkful of kidneys in my mouth than there was a loud knock on the door. It was so loud that Mrs Richards heard it in the middle room. She went to the door and an animated conversation followed. The door was closed with a bang and Mrs Richards returned to the middle room.

Half an hour later when I had finished my kidneys and my cup of tea, my landlady appeared to take the tray.

'Thank you very much,' I said. 'That was delightful. Who was that at the door?'

'It was that stupid Gloria May. She wanted to see you about the wedding. She had six little girls with her. She said she couldn't come on Friday and she'd brought her bridesmaids with her. I told her you couldn't see her because you were indeposed. So she's coming to see you before you go to the Gilbert tomorrow night.'

'I don't want to see her on her own. She must bring her fiancé with her.'

'He's in the army, isn't he? So I don't expect he will be given his French leave till the end of next week.'

I could not face another two sessions with the bride-to-be. So next morning I visited the drab terraced house, listed in the late Vicar's wedding notes as her address.

A grim-faced middle-aged replica of Gloria May opened the door, cigarette in mouth, with curlered hair and clad in grubby pinafore.

'Mrs Jones?'

She nodded and grunted the confirmation of her name.

'I've come about your daughter's wedding.'

'Oh my God! Don't say there's something wrong with the arrangements.'

'No, Mrs Jones. The wedding is fixed for twelve o'clock on Saturday week as arranged. It's just that your daughter is coming to see me tonight minus her fiancé and I must see them together to have a talk about marriage and about the service.'

'Can't you see 'er on 'er own and she can tell 'im what you said?'

'No, Mrs Jones, I'm afraid not. I must see them both.'

''E's not coming 'ome till Thursday next week.'

'In that case I'll see them both on Thursday evening at half-past six, and by the way I don't want to see the bridesmaids or anybody else. Only the two of them.'

What I did not tell the irate mother was the fact that this was my very first wedding as a solo effort. So far in my ministerial career all I had done was to act as an assistant, and not as the officiant.

Prompt at half-past six the following Thursday evening the incongruous couple appeared on the doorstep for the marriage interview. Edward Victor, a private in the Pioneer Corps, was barely five foot tall whilst Gloria May was some six inches taller. He looked petrified. She looked as disgruntled as ever.

'I 'ope you won't be long,' were her opening words. 'I've got a lot to do.'

'We'll be no longer than necessary,' I said.

They sat as far apart as they could on Mrs Richards' dining chairs brought in for the occasion.

'First of all,' I began, 'I must have all the details for the marriage register.'

'You've got those,' she snapped.

'I'm afraid I haven't. I must have your father's full names and his occupation.'

''Ave you got to 'ave that put down?'

'The law requires that his full names and occupation must be recorded.'

She looked extremely uncomfortable. The prospective bride-groom stared at her as if she were about to reveal a family skeleton.

'I'm sorry to embarrass you,' I went on. 'If it is a case of – er – his surname being different from yours or something like that, I must still have the details.'

Her colour rose.

'Look 'ere,' she shouted, 'are you saying I'm illegitimate or something?'

'I'm doing nothing of the sort,' I said as calmly as I could. 'I don't know why you are so reluctant to give his names.'

'It's because 'is parents must 'ave been stupid when they 'ad him done at the christening. If you must know 'is names are Isaiah Gladstone Thomas. Everybody calls 'im Ike. That's what they think 'is name is.'

'And what is his occupation?'

''E's a soldier in the Welsh Guards.'

When I took them through the words of the marriage service, the bride-to-be asked to be excused from obeying. I insisted that she had to say she would obey, otherwise the service would not be legal.

'Let's put it this way then,' she replied, 'I'll say it in the service that's all. After that I wouldn't obey 'im for all the tea in China.'

Edward Victor nodded his acquiescence. Apart from providing details of his father's names and occupation, he had not opened his mouth.

It was with great relief that I closed the door on them when they left.

I had an uncomfortable feeling that my first wedding was going to be a memorable one for the wrong reasons.

7

Saturday dawned bright and clear. The rain had washed the dust from the streets and the air smelt fresh in the morning sunshine.

'A nice day for a wedding,' I said to Mrs Richards as I returned with my *Times* from Thomas the paper shop.

'It was a day like this when I got married to Mr Richards here in Pontywen. He was a clerk in the colliery – well educated like my father.' The old lady looked starry eyed.

'What did your father do?'

'He was station master of Pontywen station,' she said proudly. 'Yes, we had a beautiful wedding and then we went to Llandrindod Wells for our honeymoon. First-class department to ourselves. My father arranged that. Llandrindod Wells was very posh in those days. Big hotels, full of lots of rich people. They used to come there for the water. It's full of sulphuric acid, you see.'

'That must have been dreadful to drink.'

'It was. It smelt like eggs that have declined. I wouldn't even taste it. Mr Richards did. He was very brave like that. He was badly deposed for days after.'

'I don't doubt that,' I said and settled down to *The Times* crossword.

When I arrived for the wedding there was an excited crowd of guests outside the church porch. Inside the empty church, Mr Greenfield, the organist, was playing 'Moonlight and Roses' featuring the tremolo stop.

I went down to the vestry where two diminutive privates from the Pioneer Corps were standing in a corner, apparently in a state of nervous collapse.

'Have you arranged for the ushers to give out the hymn books?' I said to Edward Victor.

He stared at me in blank amazement.

'Have you got a couple of your friends to give out books to the congregation?' I repeated. 'If you remember, I asked you on Thursday night to arrange that.'

'I – er – forgot all about it. Bert, would you get somebody to do it?'

His best man glared at him. 'All right, Eddie. 'Oo do I ask?'

'Anybody, Bert.'

Bert's boots clicked their way down the aisle.

Eddie looked terrified. He could not have been more frightened if he had been trapped in a shell hole in a fierce battle.

'You'll tell me what to do about the ring and everything, won't you, Reverend.'

'Of course I will. Just do what I tell you to do and say what I tell you to say.'

My assurance did nothing to allay his fears. Suddenly there was a hubbub inside the nave which mercifully drowned the organist's sickly rendering of 'Moonlight and Roses'.

'They're coming in,' shrieked Eddie as if the executioners were coming.

'Calm down,' I ordered. 'It will soon be over.'

'It's all right for you,' he murmured. 'You've done this many times before, I expect.'

If only you knew, I said to myself, you would be ten times more nervous.

A few minutes later Bert appeared in the vestry.

'They're giving out the books,' he informed us.

'I'd better go and check,' I said. 'You two go and sit in the front pew until the bride arrives.'

I walked down the aisle in the midst of the chattering congregation whose combined breath had the strength of a large brewery.

To my surprise, there at the church door stood a vision in white, a tall Nordic blonde, in full bridal array. The vision was in a raging temper. Attended by a large retinue of bridesmaids, flower-girls and page boys, she looked more like Queen Boadicea prepared for battle than a 'bride adorned for her husband', as the Bible has it. Her father, the Welsh Guardsman, impressive in his uniform, looked as if he would rather be on the parade ground.

'What's the matter?' I enquired.

'Matter?' she spat the word. 'My mother, that's the matter. She had a fag in her mouth when she was dressing me and it went through my veil.'

I examined the offending veil.

'I can't see anything.'

'Just like a man,' she replied between gritted teeth. 'You're not looking in the right place. 'Ere it is, by 'ere.' She pointed to a small hole, lightly decorated with nicotine.

'No one will notice that,' I ventured.

'They will,' she hissed. 'Don't worry.'

'Stay here,' I said. 'You're early and I have to put my surplice and stole on. I'll lead you down the aisle.'

'I'm not waiting long 'ere,' she replied. 'They're all staring at me.'

Her father looked at me and then looked up at the heavens. His patience had taken a battering.

When I arrived back in the vestry, I remembered that I had left my surplice and stole in St Padarn's Church. I looked in the late Vicar's cupboard only to find that his widow had removed his robes. Into the choir vestry I dashed and took one of the choirmen's surplices.

Suddenly the strains of 'Here comes the bride' filled the church. All the stops on the organ were out – sufficient even to drown the conversation in the nave. Evidently Gloria May had decided not to wait for me to emerge from the vestry.

I dived into the surplice, frantically trying to get my arms through the sleeves and discovering that the garment was on back to front. Quickly I withdrew my arms from the sleeves and swivelled the offending garment into its correct position. I dashed out into the nave.

The bride and her father were almost at the chancel steps. In the front pew sat the bridegroom and the best man, looking as if they were hiding from the military police. I motioned to them to come to the front. They looked surprised. By now the bride had passed them and was standing at the chancel step, pinioning her father's arm.

Sheepishly, the two men arose and shambled into line with

the bride and her father. The organ music stopped. The congregation ceased their loud chatter. There was a pregnant silence as the congregation and I looked at each other.

To my horror, I realised that I was standing there without the prayer book and the hymn numbers. I was frozen to the spot. A loud stage whisper from the organ stool broke the stillness of the shrine. 'Five-twenty,' it said.

'Hymn number five-twenty. Five hundred and twenty,' I intoned in a shaky voice. The organ broke into the strains of 'Love Divine' as I made a rapid exit to the vestry. I swooped up the prayer book and the couple's names from the desk and reached the chancel step by the end of the first verse.

The bride, still locked to her soldier-father's arm, stared into space. Her father was in a similar trance-like attitude. On the other hand, the bridegroom and the best man were more interested in their highly polished boots. It was not an inspiring sight.

'There's no need to hang on to your father's arm now,' I said to the bride. 'You had better pass your bouquet back to one of your bridesmaids.'

Her father performed a smart military manoeuvre, holding his arm out stiffly to allow his daughter to disengage and then stepping one pace to the left, as if on parade.

Holding her bouquet like an offensive weapon at the end of an outstretched arm, she swung round – so fast that she knocked her fifteen stone father sideways. It was a stiff-arm tackle worthy of an All-Blacks forward.

She ignored her staggering father and surveyed the bridal retinue as a colonel would have inspected his troops. To her intense annoyance, she discovered her chief bridesmaid in earnest conversation with an eligible bachelor in the second pew, on the bride's side.

'Hey, Lil,' she bawled as loud as any sergeant-major. 'Stop talking and come 'ere.' Her command drowned the few quavering voices who were murdering hymn 520. 'I told you that you were supposed to take these flowers from me.'

An embarrassed Lil grabbed the bouquet and glared at the bride. Her father had now recovered his equilibrium and was buried in a hymn book, waiting for the earth to swallow him.

Meanwhile, the unfortunate bridegroom smiled wanly at me,

as if to apologise for his wife's behaviour. His hand shook as he held a hymn book which was intended to be shared, but was ignored by the fuming virago who was about to become his wife.

The bridegroom had gone back to examining his boots when I addressed him.

'Edward Victor, wilt thou have this woman to thy wedded wife?'

I got no further than this when he raised his head and said 'yes'. I shook my head at him and continued reading the rest of the vow. There was a hush in the church as we looked at each other.

'It's "I will",' I whispered.

'Sorry,' he replied. 'Yes, I will.'

The bride glared at him.

I addressed her. 'Gloria May, wilt thou have this man to thy wedded husband.'

'I will,' she announced in militant tones.

'Who giveth this woman to be married to this man?' I said. The guardsman stepped sharply to his right, seized his daughter's left hand and barked 'I do'.

'Thank you,' I whispered to him, 'but it's the other hand I want.'

There followed an intricate pattern of hand changing when the bride's veil became entangled – as a result of which her headdress was in danger of being pulled off.

Most bridegrooms are incoherent when making their vows, sometimes through nervousness and sometimes through alcoholic antidotes for nervousness. Eddie was the most incoherent I have ever heard. I spoke to him in English. He seemed to be repeating the words in Chinese or Arabic. When I reached the last part of the vow, he did speak in English but not what I had asked him to say.

I said to him, 'and thereto I plight thee my troth.'

He shut his eyes, tried to remember and stammered 'and – er – thereto I – er – light thee my tooth.'

Gloria May's vow could be heard at the back of the church. So too were her next words.

A trickle of liquid had emerged from the direction of a small flower girl. She had been crossing her legs ever since she arrived in church. The rivulet snaked its way past the bride. She turned in a fury and slated the terrified mite. 'There you are, our Andrea, look what you've done. I told you to go before we came out.'

The best man had put the ring on the little finger of his left hand and found he had great difficulty in removing it. The bridegroom had even greater difficulty in putting it on the bride's sweaty finger – to her increasing annoyance.

'Leave it,' I said fiercely. So the ring was marooned at the top of her finger.

When I asked the couple to kneel in front of me, they adopted a Mohammedan posture of prayer. Their heads were almost on the floor and their posteriors were in the air. Apart from the unedifying spectacle which they presented, I found it very difficult to join their right hands together and read from the prayer book at the same time.

'Psalm sixty-seven,' I announced. 'We shall say the psalm in alternate verses.' I turned to the kneeling couple. 'Follow me to the altar while I say the psalm,' I whispered.

I proceeded to the sanctuary in a duologue with the organist since nobody in the congregation was interested in Psalm sixty-seven.

At the end of the Psalm I turned around to find no sign of the bride and groom at the altar rails.

I looked down to find the couple proceeding up the chancel on their knees. Under the circumstances, I thought it wiser to let them complete their journey, before launching into the prayers.

When the prayers were finished, I asked the congregation to stand. They treated this as a signal to let their hair down. The noise of movement and conversation equalled that of Cardiff Arms Park emptying after an international.

The organist tried to convey the hymn number to me. In the end, he stood up and bellowed 'Two hundred and eighty-one'.

'Hymn two hundred and eighty-one,' I echoed. 'Lead us, Heavenly Father, lead us.'

''Ow much longer?' demanded the bride.

'Just this hymn and the blessing. That's all,' I said.

'Thank God for that,' she replied, ignoring the hymn book which her little husband held in front of her.

I sang the verses as a tenor solo. It was with great relief that I shepherded the throng into the vestry. I had to carve my way through 'a wall of human flesh', in the words of W. C. Fields, to get to the desk.

'Where do I sign?' she demanded.

'I'm afraid it is the bridegroom who signs first,' I said.

'I always thought it was ladies first,' she objected.

'This is one occasion when that doesn't apply. The bridegroom has to sign on the top line.' Even my patience, which was plentiful, was running out.

She flounced out of the chair, knocking over the open bottle of Stephens' black ink. The spotless registers were spotless no longer and a polka-dot decoration appeared on the midriff of her bridal gown.

'Now look what you've done!' she screamed.

'I beg your pardon,' I said. 'You did that, not me.'

'You left the top off the bottle,' she persisted.

'Gloria!' The guardsman father, Isaiah Gladstone, had had

72

enough. He emerged from the mêlée and caught her by the shoulders. 'That's enough,' he warned her.

A blessed hush descended. I found some blotting-paper and did what I could to clean up the registers. The bride stood in a corner, shedding tears, attended by a solicitous mother. The white-faced bridegroom stood in the opposite corner in earnest conversation with his best man.

The registers were signed without further mishap. I delivered the marriage certificate to the bride who proceeded to stuff it down the front of her dress, rather than surrender it to her husband. I was presented with an envelope containing the fees by the best man. The bride's father came up to me, slipped a pound note into my hand and invited me to the reception at the British Legion Club. 'Sorry about the trouble, Padre,' he said.

'It was no trouble at all,' I replied. 'I'm afraid I can't come to the reception, I have to go elsewhere, but thank you all the same.' Another two white lies, I said to myself. My total for the week must have reached double figures.

The bride had recovered her equilibrium by now and ordered her husband to stand on her right hand side.

'I'm afraid it's the other way about,' I said.

'The curate knows,' her little husband dared to remark.

She gave him a poisonous glance and changed sides without comment. The comment would come later in the nuptial bed, if not before.

Seconds later, Mr Greenfield plunged into Mendelssohn's wedding march and I led the 'happy' couple as they moved out into a future which appeared to be far from happy.

Outside the door of the church, we were met by Humphries the Snap, the local photographer, who was as ancient as his equipment. He wore a long grey overcoat which almost trailed on the ground. His large red nose advertised his devotion to the whisky bottle.

'Shall we have one snap of the three of you together? Do you mind, Reverend?' he asked.

'Not at all,' I said, preening myself for my first wedding picture.

'Stop pushing behind,' shouted Gloria May.

'Better close the church doors,' suggested her father. The doors were closed.

'If you don't mind, Reverend, go round the other side of the bride – the rose between two – er . . . Well, there we are,' said Mr Humphries, as he retreated to his tripod and hid under the covering to peer through the lens of what seemed to be a museum exhibit rather than a camera.

'Fine,' said the muffled voice. 'Move a bit closer to the bride, Reverend.'

'I wish 'e'd 'urry up,' moaned the bride. 'It looks as if it's going to rain.'

'Fine. That's fine. Now stay as you are and smile. Smile, please, say cheese.'

Gloria May had an expression so sour it would turn fresh milk into cheese.

'Fine, thank you.'

Mr Humphries emerged from underneath his covering and I made a hasty departure by the side of the church into the vestry. There I met the organist who had come to collect his fee.

'Thank you for helping me out with the hymn numbers,' I said.

'That's all right,' he replied. 'The old Vicar would forget from time to time. He even forgot a wedding once and I had to get him out from under his car in the garage to come and take it. Mind, he was getting on then. Well, I'd better be getting back to Mrs Greenfield. She's still grieving about Billie.'

'The budgie?' I said.

'That's right. I keep telling her it was only a bird but she says she feels like a murderess. That's women for you. Well, see you tomorrow.'

I spent some time using an ink eraser, thoughtfully provided by my late Vicar, to tidy up the registers. It must have been a half-hour later that I went to the front door to lock it.

Outside the church, the wedding party was still being photographed. Overtopping the noisy chatter of the guests, came the shrill voice of Gloria May.

'Come on, our Mam. Stand by yer. Gran, stop talking to Uncle Will and stand next to our Mam. Where are you going, Andrea? Stand by there. You've been enough trouble for today, thank you.'

As I passed the church gate, the elderly photographer emerged. He had deserted his tripod and hidden behind a tree.

If it wasn't for the money, I'd pack up and go home,' he said to me. 'As it is, I've come down here to cool off. That girl needs a kick up the khyber, if you'll pardon the expression.'

'I will indeed,' I replied. 'As a matter of fact, I had the same feeling about her during the service.'

'Do you smoke, young man?' he asked, producing a packet of Players.

'No thank you.'

He lit up and blew a cloud of smoke after his first puff.

'Women!' He spat the word and stared into space.

'Where's the photographer?' shrieked the bride.

'See what I mean,' he said, and disappeared up the church path, discarding the cigarette as he went.

Mr Humphries' comment on women prompted me to call at the Vicarage to see how Mrs Llewellyn was coping with the business of removal. To my surprise the large Pickfords van was already making its way up the Vicarage drive. The widow, a forlorn figure, was standing on the front doorstep watching its departure.

'I didn't expect to see the van going so early,' I said to her.

'That's Pickfords for you. You always get what you pay for and Pickford's are the best. It's on its way to the storage department. I expect I shall have to get rid of most of the furniture.' Her bottom lip quivered for a second.

'I'm glad you've come,' she went on. 'You can have the keys. I know you'll look after them. By the way, I've left a few of the Vicar's books for you.'

'That's very kind of you, Mrs Llewellyn,' I replied, with tongue in cheek. The bulk of his library was up to date in the early years of this century.

'Well, if you don't mind, I must get back and have one last look around to see if everything is all right. The taxi is coming for me to take me to the station in ten minutes' time. I've arranged to have the place scrubbed out and cleaned on Monday. I don't want that John Whittaker saying the Vicarage was left like a pigsty. Though from what I gather, his housekeeper might make it one.'

That was news to me. So there would not be a Vicar's wife this time.

She shook hands with me. It would be the last time I would

see her. No longer did she look a dragoness. She was simply a frail, little old lady whose empire had come to an end – a sad end.

'Goodbye, Mrs Llewellyn,' I said. 'I hope you soon find somewhere to settle in Bournemouth.'

'Time will tell,' she replied and went back into the empty Vicarage.

I wondered what the house would be like once it was full of somebody else's furniture and without a vicaress in charge. At least, I said to myself, I would not have to fight a war on two fronts. There would only be Father John Whittaker to contend with, not another Mrs Llewellyn as well.

8

'We've got to do something special for Christmas,' said Charles Wentworth-Baxter at our Monday morning meeting. His enthusiasm spelt trouble. I had a vivid recollection of his decoration of the sanctuary floor at the Harvest Service in St Padarn's. He had arranged biscuits to form the text 'God is Love' forgetting that the clergy had to move about freely to distribute the sacrament.

'Since it is only three weeks next Tuesday,' I replied testily, 'I don't think there's much we can do.'

'Look, Fred. It is the first Christmas since the war. I know we've still got rationing and all that. Can't we have a Christmas tree and dress it up? And have a midnight service?'

'You must be joking. We have been informed by our Vicar-to-be that there must be no alteration of the status quo until he arrives. In any case can you imagine the old stick-in-the-muds in the parish church agreeing to it?'

'But you could do it in St Padarn's. You're in charge of it. Besides, if we have a midnight service there then we can both be together for St Padarn's and the parish church.'

'I thought there was method in your madness, Charles. What you mean is that you will be able to avoid being in sole charge at the big services, you devious curate. In any case, where are we going to get a tree? It has to be a big one if it is going to be in church. Let's think it over.'

After he had gone, I began to warm to the idea. I was in charge of St Padarn's and I was doing nothing to change the services in the parish church. However, if anything was to be done it had to be done as soon as possible.

That afternoon, I was taking a funeral service in the churchyard. After the burial I mentioned to Full-Back Jones that I was thinking of getting a Christmas tree for St Padarn's.

His face lit up. 'I can 'elp you there, Reverend. I know a dealer up the valley.'

'Will it be expensive?' I asked. 'We can't afford a big price.'

'You can 'ave it for nothing. 'E owes me some favours anyway. Keep it under your 'at, though. It's between you and me.'

I thanked him profusely and he went off like a dog with two tails to his task of filling in the grave.

Later in the week at the Gilbert and Sullivan music rehearsal I asked the company if anyone knew of someone who would lend us lights for the Christmas tree. The first hand up belonged to Eleanor.

'Please sir,' she said mockingly, 'I'm sure we can lend ours. I'm getting a bit big for Christmas trees and pillow cases.'

There were three other offers and Bertie Owen said that he knew somebody at work who would lend us a length of cable for the wiring.

After evensong at St Padarn's I announced that Christmas would be celebrated with a Christmas tree and a midnight service. The idea of a Christmas tree met with universal approval. The midnight Communion service was an innovation welcomed excitedly by the younger members of the congregation but regarded with suspicion by some of the older worshippers.

'Suppose somebody drunk staggered in off the streets,' said Mrs Annie Jones, in a shower of spit. She had forgotten to put her false teeth back in her mouth after the last hymn. It was her usual practice to sing minus her teeth which would be placed in her handbag during the hymns.

'Don't worry about that, Annie.' Bertie Owen was on his feet. 'I'll see that any intruder will be evicted before he can cause any trouble. I'll put a couple of sidesmen on special duty for that.'

She accepted his assurance with a nod and daintily replaced her dentures.

'I don't like this idea,' objected Mrs Collier, leading soprano. 'It will spoil the seven o'clock service which is always packed. We always have "The Holy City" as an anthem. I've been singing the solo in that for years and years.'

'There's no reason to stop singing "The Holy City" if we do

have a service at midnight,' I said. 'Mind, I don't know why you sing it at Christmas. It has nothing to do with the birth of Jesus. Perhaps you would like to sing the solo in a Christmas carol instead.'

'What a good idea,' commented Idris the Milk, winking at me with the eye which was hidden from Mrs Collier's gaze. 'You could sing "Silent Night". It would be very appropriate at midnight.'

'If it comes to that,' interjected Annie Jones, 'we could sing quite a few carols, with other soloists as well.' Annie Jones was Mrs Collier's rival in the soprano stakes.

'This is not the place to be discussing what has to be sung at the service.' I decided to end any further provocation of Mrs Collier whose face was growing more crimson every minute. 'I simply wanted to inform you that we're having a midnight service and a Christmas tree. With only two weeks to go we have to move quickly in our preparations to let everybody know.'

'You can say that again,' riposted Mrs Collier. 'Everybody will be expecting the seven o'clock morning service.'

'Posters.' Bertie Owen was on his feet again. 'Posters. We'll have 'em in as many houses as we can – and word of mouth, of course.'

'What about getting something in the paper?' suggested Idris. 'You know. Curate's bold experiment.'

'I don't think that's necessary,' I said quickly. If Father Whittaker read that news item in the newspaper, he would be calling at my digs the next minute.

'If I were you,' advised Eleanor when we had our usual Sunday evening date after service, 'I should make peace with Madame Collier and let her sing her "Holy City", for this year at any rate. You'll need all the co-operation you can get if you want to make a success of your midnight venture.'

'Your very word is my command, princess,' I replied.

Next morning I called at the Collier abode. The lady of the house appeared at the door looking like a superannuated member of a harem. Her curlered hair was hidden under a turban while her scrawny body was covered with a pinafore, revealing bare arms and legs. A cloud of steam emanated from the open door of the kitchen. It was washing day. Her face, flushed with the heat of her laundering, displayed a mixture of suspicion and surprise.

'I wonder if I might have a word with you, Mrs Collier,' I said.

'I'm hardly in a state to receive visitors.' The tone was acid. 'You'd better come in the front room.'

I was ushered into the parlour.

'If you don't mind, I'd better go and shut the kitchen door to stop the steam going through the house.'

She disappeared for a few minutes and came back wearing a cardigan buttoned up around the neck as a concession to modesty.

'What can I do for you?' She sat on the edge of her Rexine armchair, making it obvious that the interview was going to be short.

'It's just to say that I should be pleased if you would sing "The Holy City" at the midnight service. Obviously it has been part of Christmas in St Padarn's for some years.'

Her expression changed. The frown gave place to something like a smile.

'Well when you've been singing that piece every Christmas for years, it becomes part of it, as you say. Anyway, thank you. We'll all have to do our best to get a good crowd, won't we? After all, it's just a fortnight tomorrow, isn't it?'

'We'll get plenty of posters out and about, Bertie Owen is seeing to that. I think there'll be a good number of people there.'

'I hope so. Would you like a quick cup of tea, Mr Secombe? It won't take a minute.'

'Just a quick one then. I don't want to hold up your work. In any case, I've got to get around quite a few houses.'

'You sound like Mr Williams the insurance. He's always saying that.' With that attempt at banter, she went off to make the tea.

She reappeared with a tray containing two cups of tea, milk jug, sugar bowl and a book of raffle tickets.

'I'm afraid I'm out of biscuits. Would you like to buy a raffle ticket? Threepence each or five for a shilling. Mr Collier's been given a book to sell for the British Legion's Christmas draw. First prize is a bottle of whisky and second prize is a chicken.'

'I wouldn't want the first prize but I would certainly like the second and so would Mrs Richards.'

I bought five tickets, drank my tea and left Mrs Collier a much happier person than when she opened the door to me.

As the days went by, Bertie's homemade posters seemed to be in every other house in the St Padarn's district of Pontywen. They suffered from a significant defect. It was impossible to read the wording from a distance of more than three feet. However, Bertie was more than pleased with his efforts.

'I've been up till midnight working on the posters every night for a week and I'll tell you what – Pontywen is flooded with them now.'

This was his proud boast at the last Gilbert and Sullivan rehearsal before Christmas. He was so excited that Aneurin, the musical director, had to reprimand him more than once for disrupting the proceedings.

'I don't know what he's bragging about,' said Idris. 'It looks as if half the houses in Pontywen have put up the white flag. You can't see a word on the white paper.'

The excitement was not confined to Bertie. It had Charles Wentworth-Baxter in its grip also.

After the rehearsal he took me aside.

'I've got some surprise decorations for the tree.' He was like a small child, wide-eyed in anticipation of Christmas.

'Don't tell me, Charles. It's a packet of biscuits which you're going to use to spell out Merry Christmas at the front of the tree.'

'Come off it, Fred. They're decorations to hang on the tree. By the way, when is the tree coming?'

'Full-Back Jones tells me it will arrive tomorrow. So we'll put it in position on Christmas Eve and decorate it then.'

'Can't we do it on Saturday? There are only two more days to Christmas after that.'

'Certainly not. Next Sunday is the Fourth Sunday in Advent. You don't celebrate Christmas beforehand even if the shops do.'

When Eleanor drove me back to Mount Pleasant View afterwards, she remarked about Charles Wentworth-Baxter's immaturity.

'He's a Peter Pan,' she said. 'I don't think he will ever grow up enough to have charge of a parish.'

'It's amazing what the grace of God can achieve,' I replied.

'All I can say about that is that it will have to be equivalent to getting a camel through the eye of a needle. So let's talk about reality. You are invited to tea with us on Christmas Day. There will be a few family guests and friends there as well. It should be a nice relaxing evening when you won't be grilled by my mother.'

'I was hoping I'd see you on Christmas Day. That's marvellous. Thank you.' I kissed her.

'Hold on,' she said. 'You'll see me on Christmas Day anyway. I'm coming to your Midnight Service, if it's only to see Charles's decorations.'

'It's going to be a wonderful Christmas,' I proclaimed.

I spoke too soon.

Friday came and by late Friday afternoon there was no sign of the tree from Full-Back Jones. I called round at his hovel. He was not in. His neighbours said that they had not seen him since early afternoon. I began to panic. If the gravedigger failed to keep his promise there was no hope of getting another tree.

When I arrived at my digs, I found Mrs Richards, beaming with delight.

'What do you think?' she said. 'The man from that Foreign Legion club has been here. You've won the chicken in their Christmas drawing. I haven't had chicken since before the war. The price of chicken is gastronomic. My husband always used to say that having chicken for dinner was the highest light at Christmas. The man is bringing it here first thing on Christmas Eve.'

She looked at me quizzically.

'You don't seem very pleased,' she commented.

'Of course I'm pleased we are going to have chicken for our Christmas dinner – but are we going to have a Christmas tree for our Christmas service? It hasn't arrived yet and no one knows where Full-Back Jones is. Perhaps he's in hiding because his friend the dealer didn't provide the goods.

'Don't worry, Mr Secombe,' the old lady said reassuringly. 'I don't think he'll backfire on his promise.'

She was right. At nine o'clock that night there was a knock on the door. It was the tree provider.

'You'll find the tree at the back of the church.' He grinned his toothless grin. 'I'll have a barrel for you tomorrow for to

82

put it in.' He put a dirty finger to his mouth. 'Keep it under your 'at.' With that admonition, he was down the steps and away.

Next morning I went around to the church to inspect the tree. It was enormous. Full-Back could never have carried it there. He must have brought it on a lorry. His friend the dealer was indeed generous.

By now there had been six offers of lights for the decoration of our set piece. I was beginning to catch the Charles Wentworth-Baxter Christmas fever and was sorely tempted to advance the festival to the fourth Sunday in Advent by putting up the tree that day.

However the promised barrel did not materialise until late Saturday evening and the temptation was not put to the test.

While the choir were engaged in a rehearsal of 'The Holy City', Bertie Owen buttonholed me for a discussion on where the tree was to be placed. His normally florid face was now purple with excitement.

'It's got to be up in the front for everybody to see it. And it can't be too far away from the socket because I haven't got all that amount of a lead to play with.'

In the end it was decided to place it at the side where the bible lectern was situated.

'I've told everybody to bring their lights by eleven o'clock tomorrow,' I said to Bertie.

'That'll just about give me time,' he replied.

'Bertie, the service doesn't begin until eleven-thirty at night. That's more than twelve hours.'

'I know that, Mr Secombe. But don't forget there's six lots of lights to be strung together and I want to do it nicely. Then there's lots of other things to do as well, like decorating the barrel and putting things on the tree.'

Christmas Eve was beginning to lose its attraction for me. Several hours of Bertie fussing over the tree was not a pleasant prospect, not to mention the threat of Charles's 'surprise' decorations.

So it was with a certain amount of foreboding that I arose from my bed on the eve of Christ's nativity. Mrs Richards was all agog over the Christmas chicken.

'I hope it's plucked,' she said. 'I can't stand having to withdraw all those feathers. We had one the first Christmas we were married. Mr Richards had to help me in the end. He was so good. He even got his razor to shave off all the rubble.'

We were still at the breakfast table when there was a knock at the door.

'I expect it's the chicken,' I said. 'I'd better go and collect my prize.'

I opened the door to be confronted by a little man, trilby hatted and wearing a scruffy raincoat. He was holding by its feet which had been tied together, a live cockerel which appeared to have outlived its normal span in somebody's back yard. It was too feeble to struggle.

'Your prize, Mr Secombe,' he announced. 'With the compliments of the club.'

'Is this for burial?' I asked.

'Not at all,' he said indignantly. 'We like to bring it fresh, like. Not something that's been killed days ago.'

'If you don't mind me saying so, this one looks as if it's going to die of natural causes any minute now.'

'Sorry, Mr Secombe. I can't stay 'ere to argue with you. I'm due back at the club.'

With that he pushed the two ancient feet into my hand and vanished down the street.

I closed the door and stood for a minute in the hall, wondering how I was going to face my landlady. The bird remained absolutely passive as if resigned to dying after a long and enjoyable life. I decided that the only course open to me was to make Mrs Richards laugh. I flung open the middle-room door and exclaimed,

'My prize!'

The suddenness of my attempt at humour produced a resurrection in the fowl. It flapped its wings and managed a couple of stifled squawks.

Far from laughing, Mrs Richards was petrified. She went for cover in the corner by the dresser.

'Take that out of here,' she shouted, 'before it jumps out of your hand.'

I was through the room and out into the back yard at the speed of light.

By now the bird had suffered a relapse after its brief revival.

I laid it on the ground. The creature made no attempt to move. Then for safety's sake, I shut it in the late Mr Richards' greenhouse, in case it made a miraculous recovery.

When I arrived back in the middle room, the old lady was seated at the breakfast table, her face as white as her clean tablecloth.

'I'm sorry, Mrs Richards,' I said. 'I shouldn't have done that. Believe it or not, I was trying to make you laugh rather than cry at my so-called prize.'

'That Foreign Legion lot and their drawing. I was so looking forward to our Christmas dinner.' She was almost in tears.

'Perhaps it won't taste too bad if you cook it a lot,' I suggested.

'Somebody's got to kill it first. I can't, that's certain.' She looked at me.

'Nor me either. I could shout "Boo" behind its back and it might die of fright.'

There was a glimmer of a smile on her face.

'I know what I'll do,' I went on. 'I'll go and see Full-Back Jones. He'll kill it for us, I'm sure.'

'That's a good idea, Mr Secombe. He's a bit of a poaching man. So he's bound to know what to do.'

'Found the barrel?' said the gravedigger, when I called at his house. 'Just the size for that big tree.'

'Thank you very much,' I replied. 'Could you do me one more favour?'

'What's that?'

'I've won a chicken in the British Legion raffle but it's alive and I want somebody to kill it.'

'No trouble at all. Be with you now.'

Ten minutes later Full-Back Jones entered the greenhouse while Mrs Richards and I kept out of sight – neither of us wished to witness the slaughter.

It seemed only seconds before he was back in the house with the corpse.

'Easy,' he said. 'That bird 'ad 'is pension book years ago. Should be straightforward plucking that one. Its feathers should drop off 'im. It's a wonder 'e isn't bald.'

'I hope those feathers will come off like that,' replied Mrs Richards. 'There's so much to do and I won't have the time to dally dilly with it.'

'You see,' Full-Back assured her.

When I arrived at St Padarn's there was the usual organised chaos created by Bertie Owen. Ladies were scurrying around the church with holly and evergreens of various kinds – Bertie was acting as foreman while some sidesmen he had recruited were attempting to get the tree into the barrel.

'Now the only way we're going to do this, boys, is to put the barrel on its side like the tree, then shove it in. Two of you get the barrel upright slowly while the other two do the same with the tree.'

That was easier said than done; after several abortive attempts to get the tree in position, Bertie decided that the men had better have a break.

'It isn't a break we need,' said Llew Jenkins, a retired miner, 'it's a bloody crane. Much more of this and we'll all 'ave 'ernias.'

'Why don't you manoeuvre the tree and barrel to the foot of the pulpit?' I suggested. 'If you get some rope, with two of you up in the pulpit, you could haul the tree up into position in no time. Then you could move the barrel slowly across to the other side of the chancel when everything was done.'

'Well done, Curate. It's about time we 'ad some sense 'ere.' Llew glared at Bertie Owen.

A quarter of an hour later, Percy Shoemaker, son of Idris the Milk, appeared with a length of rope borrowed from Thomas the Haulage. Soon the tree was erect and the barrel filled with bricks and stones to hold it in place.

'What a massive tree,' exclaimed Eleanor when she arrived with her contribution of fairy lights.

'"Full-Back" and his friend have done us proud,' I said.

She stared at it for a while and then took me aside.

'I don't want to dampen your enthusiasm,' she whispered, 'but Will Book and Pencil was telling me this morning that the Forestry Commission have reported that some of their trees have been – er – forcibly removed.'

My enthusiasm vanished as light dawned on the darkness of my ignorance – a red light.

'So that's why the tree was delivered at night – not to mention the barrel. I expect that was forcibly removed too, from the yard at the back of the Red Lion.'

86

'You realise you can be charged with being a receiver of stolen goods.'

I gulped.

'But I didn't know they were stolen.'

'That's what they all say.'

The look of mock censure on her face gave way to a smile.

'Don't worry, love. I'm sure Will Book and Pencil won't come and take away your tree. How many people know it's a "gift" from Full-Back Jones?'

'Only you, Charles and Mrs Richards.'

'In that case you have nothing to fear. Just carry on with the decoration. Speaking of which here comes your Peter Pan colleague. I must be off.'

She squeezed my hand and went through the side door of the church.

Charles Wentworth-Baxter was carrying a large suitcase. His face was lit with a seraphic beam of happiness. The surprise was about to be revealed.

He sat down in the front pew and opened his case.

'Here we are,' he said proudly.

He produced numerous creations made out of cardboard, covered with silver paper. They had no form nor comeliness.

'What on earth are these?' I asked.

'They're angels and I've made the archangel Gabriel to go on the top of the tree.' He extricated a large monstrosity and held it in front of my face as if it were a masterpiece of creative art.

'I've made holes through each of them and put cotton through them to hang on the branches.'

'Who inspired you, Charles? Picasso or Epstein?'

He stared at me, unsure whether I had paid him a compliment or insulted him.

'Well, they will certainly be a talking point,' I added.

'Thank you, Fred,' he replied, deciding that I had seen something profound in them.

'What are these things?' said Bertie Owen in bewilderment.

'They are angels,' explained Charles, looking at me as if he despaired of the ignorance of the uncultured.

By ten o'clock that night the angels had joined the fairy lights to celebrate the advent of St Padarn's first Christmas tree. Bertie Owen was exhausted but triumphant. Hour after hour, perched precariously on a stepladder, he had worked to link up the fairy lights. Eventually when his toils were complete and he switched on the lights, he was overwhelmed with the success of his technical genius.

'They're all on!' he shouted in disbelief.

By eleven-thirty, it was standing room only in St Padarn's.

Bertie came into the vestry as I was about to say the vestry prayer.

'Mr Secombe, I've checked those who've come in and I can't see anybody the worse for wear. Anyway, I've got two good men on the door now and they'll stop any drunk from entering. So don't worry.'

The atmosphere was electric. There never was such singing in St Padarn's. They raised the roof with 'O come all faithful'.

As the prayers began, there was a respectful silence and so it continued until Mrs Collier began her anthem.

'Last night as I was sleeping, I had a dream so fair,' she sang.

We heard no more about her dream because at that moment the lights went out and the organ ceased to function.

There was an eerie silence, only to be shattered by a shout from Bertie, 'Don't panic, it's only a fuse.'

'Nobody's panicking, Mr Owen,' I said quietly. 'If you will go to the vestry and mend the fuse, we'll carry on with the service. In the meantime, we shall sit and sing from memory "Away in a manger".'

With the aid of somebody's cigarette lighter, Bertie made his way into the vestry.

The unaccompanied singing of the carol was a triumph. Most of the congregation seemed to know the words while the harmonies supplied by the choir gave the necessary depth to the music.

Emboldened by the success, I announced that we would render 'Hark the Herald Angels Sing'. Unfortunately I pitched the note too high. By the time we reached 'Joyful all ye nations, rise' most of the sopranos gave up the struggle. 'Join the triumph of the skies' was attempted by two or three ladies shrieking the impossible. 'With the angelic hosts proclaim' was left to the angelic hosts. The earthbound vocalists had surrendered.

At that moment there was a blaze of light. It was one of the

few occasions in Pontywen when I was grateful for the presence of Bertie Owen.

The rest of the service was uninterrupted and the consensus of opinion was an enthusiastic approval of the midnight venture. Charles was elated. So was Bertie.

I saw Eleanor briefly.

'Did you enjoy the service?' I asked.

'Very much so,' she replied. 'St Padarn's will never be the same again. What with Charles's attempt at modern art and Bertie's attack on the electricity supply, not to mention the strangulated hernia in "Hark the Herald".'

'You are mocking me, Eleanor Davies.'

'What makes you think that, Frederick Thomas Secombe? Honestly, it was a warm, exciting service. I thought your few words about peace on earth at the end of 1945 very moving. Merry Christmas, my dear. I can't kiss you here. I shall do that at three-thirty p.m. when I pick you up.'

'Merry Christmas, my love,' I said.

I went into the vestry to disrobe. Bertie was buzzing around like a demented bumble bee while Charlie Hughes, the other warden, assisted by Idris the Milk, was counting the collection.

'Must be record takings,' enthused Bertie.

Suddenly outside in the chancel I heard the unmistakable tones of Will Book and Pencil.

My heart missed several beats.

Into the vestry he strode, helmet tucked under his arm.

'Any trouble tonight?' he enquired.

'None at all,' I assured him.

'Good,' he replied. 'I was going to keep an eye on things outside just in case of drunks but I got called to a couple of punch ups in the town.'

'I had everything under control,' said Bertie.

As he went out of the vestry, the constable paused and looked at the tree.

'That's a fine tree, Mr Secombe,' he remarked.

My heart missed several more beats.

'Yes, it was given by a great friend of the church who wished to remain anonymous.'

'Good to have rich friends like that,' said Will Book and Pencil. 'You must introduce me one day. I could do with a friend like that. Merry Christmas.'

'That's the best of knowing the right people,' I replied with my tongue firmly in my cheek. 'Merry Christmas, Constable.'

'What's that you are whistling?' asked Bertie Owen as we walked away from the church a little later on.

'It's called "When you come to the end of a perfect day".'

'That's not a carol.'

'No, but it's often sung at the end of Christmas Eve.'

'Well, I never knew that before,' said Bertie.

9

It seemed no time at all after Christmas that the new incumbent was inducted to the living of Pontywen on a cold February day. Despite the sleet and the bitter wind, the parish church was full for the service. The congregation was keen to inspect what the Patronage Board had thrust upon them.

'Before I commend your new Vicar as a worthy successor to your late beloved priest, Canon Llewellyn,' said the Bishop in his address, 'I must thank the Reverend Fred Secombe for his care of the parish in the interregnum. Considering the brevity of his experience he has shown a sense of responsibility beyond his years.'

This episcopal tribute was received with a scowl by Father Whittaker who was anxious to hear his own virtues paraded for the benefit of the congregation not those of his underling. It boded ill for the Monday morning meeting in the Vicarage, at which, Charles and I were informed, the 'pastoral strategy' would be unveiled.

So on Monday it was not without a certain amount of misgiving that Charles and I made our way to the parish church where we were to say matins together with our overlord, prior to the 'strategy' meeting.

He met us at the church door, clad in cassock and cape.

'Where are your cassocks?' he demanded. 'From now on I want you to wear your cassocks to church for our daily service.'

The mention of cassocks and daily services caused the blood to drain from Charles's cheeks. It so unnerved him that when he read the first lesson from the Old Testament which included the ten commandments, he stammered his way into a spoonerism. 'Thou shalt not covet thy neighbour's wife, nor his servant, nor his maid, nor his ax nor his oss.'

I suppressed a giggle. However, when the Vicar proceeded to say the prayers, the urge to indulge in unseemly mirth became almost overwhelming.

'Oolmighty Gad' was but one example of distorted speech in his approach to the throne of heaven. To make matters worse for anyone with a sense of humour was the automatic smile which accompanied the words of the prayers. It indicated that he had a 'pally with the deity' relationship. If I were to survive a curacy with this man for any length of time, self control would be essential.

Matins over, we were escorted to the Vicarage where already there were signs that the old order had given place to the new – for the worse. No longer did the smell of polish predominate as we entered the hall. Instead our nostrils were assaulted by the smell of fish heads being boiled for the housekeeper's two cats. Mrs Lilywhite, a widow, was named inappropriately. Her lack of care for her person was on a par with her lack of care for the house. She had one big plus mark – a complete disinterest in the parish.

'Mrs Lilywhite, can we have three coffees in the study?' bawled the Vicar on entering his domain.

'You'll have to hold on for a minute. I'm doing the washing.' The housekeeper had a strong pair of lungs.

Charles and I looked at each other. At least there were going to be compensations for whatever we were going to suffer from our new employer.

We were ushered into the study where there had been a complete transformation. Gone were the floor to ceiling bookshelves, groaning under the weight of indigestible tomes. Apart from one large set of shelves, the newly decorated walls were plastered with religious paintings and framed photographs of clerics. One of them seemed to be of the Pope in his red cap.

It reminded me of a story I heard once about a Roman Catholic family, living in Llanelly, who had become backsliders. The priest decided that they needed a visit. He was taken into the front room by the lady of the house.

'Mrs Murphy, you have not been attending mass or confessions,' he said.

'We've all been busy with one thing or another,' replied the lady.

The priest looked up and saw the photograph of a red capped personage in a place of honour on the mantelpiece.

'It's something that you hold the Holy Father in reverence,' he observed, pointing at the photograph.

'Excuse me, Father,' came the reply, 'but that's Albert Jenkins.'

Albert Jenkins was the famous Welsh International rugby player pictured proudly wearing his cap.

My reverie was ended by a call to order from Father Whittaker.

'Right, now let's get down to business.' He opened a drawer in his desk and produced a file of papers which he placed at the foot of a large crucifix which occupied the central position. He had an obsession for crucifixes. There was one on the mantelpiece, one hanging on the wall and one hanging from the belt around his cassock.

'Before we go any further, let's get first things first. Sunday services. I shall be anchored in the parish church. You, Secombe, are anchored already in St Padarn's. That means that you, Wentworth-Baxter, will be anchored in Llanhyfryd.'

'Father!' came a call from the kitchen.

He rose from his chair and stalked indignantly out into the hall.

'Who does he think he is?' said Charles. 'Chaplain to the Missions to Seamen?'

Father's head appeared around the door. 'Milk and sugar for both?' he grunted.

'Please,' we said in unison.

Seconds later he was back at his desk.

'As I was saying, you will be at Llanhyfryd, Wentworth-Baxter. That means you will have to learn to drive my car, if you don't already know how. We can't afford to hire taxis.'

Charles looked petrified.

'I've never driven in my life, Vicar.'

'Then I shall have to teach you. When you leave this morning go down to the Post Office and get a provisional licence. This afternoon I want the three of us to visit Sir David Jones-Williams and you shall have your first lesson on the way there.'

Evidently Father Whittaker was a social climber and wished to impress the squire by bringing an entourage. What he did not realise was the fact that I was *persona non grata* with Sir David after colliding with his car during the summer. Furthermore the local worthy was a liverish gentleman who detested change of any kind. Vestments and Anglo-Catholic ritual would give him apoplexy.

'Vestments,' said the Vicar, as if reading my mind. 'Before long I shall introduce them in Pontywen as part of a plan to raise the level of worship. Ultimately I should like to see incense and sanctuary bells in all three churches.'

By now Charles had a glazed look in his eyes.

'If you don't mind my saying so, Vicar,' I felt I had to speak my mind before he went any further in disclosing his plans, 'I am afraid you will empty all three churches with these changes.'

He glared at me through his horn-rimmed spectacles and quoted the Scriptures.

'He who is not with me is against me.'

'That's what I call stating the obvious, Vicar,' I said. 'The trouble is that all your congregations will be against you.'

'And my curates as well, by the sound of it.' He was beginning to lose his temper.

'Let me put it this way. Vestments will not worry me but when you begin smells and bells, I shall go elsewhere.'

'Shall we drop this subject for the time being?' he snapped. 'Now then, next week we shall begin a door to door visitation of every house in Pontywen.' He patted the file of papers on his desk. 'I have prepared these forms which will give details of every person in the house, age, denomination and whether baptised or confirmed. When the parochial survey is complete, we shall have an exact picture of the parish and the task that lies ahead of us.'

There was a loud knock on the door.

'Come in,' he shouted.

Mrs Lilywhite entered, carrying a tin tray on which were three cups, generously filled with coffee which was flowing over the brim and into the saucers beneath. She wore a less than clean pinafore pinned together over her ample bosom. Grey haired and rose cheeked with a cheerful smile she sweetened an atmosphere which was decidedly sour, despite the smell of boiled fish-heads she brought with her.

Charles and I sipped our coffee while the Vicar proceeded to give us detailed instruction on how we were to conduct our door-to-door survey.

'Be here sharp at two-fifteen both of you,' were his parting words as we left.

'Yes, teacher,' said Charles when the Vicarage door was closed. 'What am I going to do, Fred? I'm hopeless with machines of any kind.'

The gleaming Austin Big Seven stood at the side of the house. A new garage was due to be installed in a few weeks' time, we had been informed.

'I tell you one thing, Charles. This car will be a lot easier to drive than the Canon's old Morris. At least it will have brakes that work. Don't worry.'

At two-fifteen prompt, we walked down the Vicarage drive. Charles was like a condemned man on his way to the scaffold. The dreaded machine was parked outside the door. My colleague stared at it with fearful eyes, as if it would attack him at any moment.

Before I could ring the door bell, Father Whittaker emerged, looking at his wristwatch.

'Just in time,' he observed.

'You said two-fifteen on the dot, Vicar. We couldn't be more on the dot than this.'

He grunted in reply.

'Wentworth-Baxter. In the front seat alongside me, please.'

It was obvious that he was savouring my colleague's hyphenated name.

I got in the back seat without waiting to be ordered there.

Charles stared at the instrument panel as if mesmerised. How was he going to keep an eye on these gadgets and drive at the same time, let alone control the pedals with his feet and steer the wheel with his hands. I knew the feeling from my own experience.

We drove up the drive to the gate which we had closed behind us.

'Open the gate,' came the command to Charles.

He got out, leaving the car door open, undid the latch and pushed the heavy gate to one side.

The next second the Vicar launched the machine at the entrance like a missile from its ramp. The open door struck the gate post with a resounding clang, and developed a list to starboard, while the bottom hinges of the door parted company with the car.

There was a pregnant silence.

'Sorry, Vicar,' said Charles.

Father's self-control was having a battle. He got out to inspect the damage.

'Never leave the car door open again, Wentworth-Baxter. Got that. Never again. It looks as if it will hold until I take it to the garage tomorrow. Now get in while I close it.'

Charles got in, a pale shadow of his former self. He closed his eyes, apparently praying that the earth would swallow him.

The Vicar drove a few yards out on the road and stopped.

'Secombe, would you mind closing the gate, please?' Evidently he had decided not to issue orders to me.

Once the car was outside the town, we stopped on a lonely road.

'This is where you take over, Wentworth-Baxter.' Charles moved to open his door.

'Don't you do that!' shouted his driving instructor. 'I'll get out and open it while you move into the driving seat.'

The Vicar opened his door and got out. My colleague attempted to move into the driving seat, and by an ingenious manoeuvre trapped the gear lever inside the leg of his trousers. In the meantime the Vicar had opened the passenger door gingerly and deposited himself in the front seat, causing Charles to sit on his employer's right knee, with the gear lever still sticking up his trousers giving the impression of a badly broken leg.

It took another minute or so to disentangle the lever to the great amusement of the audience in the back of the car.

'Now then,' said the Vicar to a distraught Charles sitting in the driving seat, 'that which stuck up your trouser leg is called the gear lever.'

Painstakingly he explained the use of the clutch, the gear lever, the accelerator and the brake.

'Right, let's see you drive,' he ordered.

After four or five attempts to start without stalling the engine,

Charles drove off in a shuddering car. The perspiration on his forehead was running down his cheeks, despite the cold February weather.

He had crawled in third gear for about half a mile when the gates of Sir David Jones-Williams' residence, Llanhyfryd Hall, appeared.

'This is it,' I said.

'Pull into the side and put your foot on the brake,' commanded the Vicar.

Charles pulled into the side nicely but put his foot on the accelerator instead of the brake. We shot into a ditch at the side of the road. It was a deep ditch. Father Whittaker's ten gallon hat tilted over his face, bringing his spectacles off his nose and into his lap. From underneath the hat came unseemly language, suggesting that my colleague was some kind of an idiot.

'Don't just sit there!' the Vicar shouted after removing the hat from his mouth. 'Get out, man!'

Charles got out – only to find his feet sinking into a bog which had already begun to cover the tyres. Any minute now, I thought, my colleague's prayer would be answered. The earth would have swallowed him, plus the Vicar's car, the Vicar and me.

'It's very boggy,' said Charles.

'That's all we need,' exploded the Vicar. He pushed open the passenger door which lurched to one side and embedded itself in the soggy bank. He swivelled round to the side of the seat, his little legs dangling in mid air. He surveyed the morass beneath as if he were marooned in mid-Atlantic.

'Now, what do we do?' He wailed the question to the heavens, apparently addressing the Almighty, rather than his curates.

The Lord heard his cry and straightaway sent an angel of mercy. It was in the ample form of Islwyn Jenkins, tenant farmer on the Squire's estate and an enthusiastic member of my Gilbert and Sullivan society. He was driving his tractor from a nearby field.

'Well, Mr Secombe,' he said, gazing down from his tractor seat. 'Fallen by the wayside, is it?'

Father Whittaker had no sense of humour. Even if he'd had one it would have been sorely tried by that remark.

'This is our new Vicar, Islwyn. He was giving Charles a driving lesson.'

'Pleased to meet you, Vicar.' The farmer grinned. 'You're not having much success with your efforts.'

'Good heavens, man!' Father Whittaker's face was scarlet. 'This is no time for tomfoolery. Get some help to pull us out of here.'

'No offence,' replied the farmer. 'Don't get out. Your friend has already got his feet wet,' pointing to a forlorn Charles whose shoes had almost disappeared in the mire.

'He's not my friend.' Our employer said this with some feeling. 'He's my curate.'

'I think you'll like Pontywen. We're not a bad lot are we, Mr Secombe?'

The Vicar's patience snapped.

'Go and get some help, will you?' he barked.

'No need,' said our deliverer cheerfully. He jumped down from his tractor, and pulled out a length of rope from under the driving seat.

'Always keep this for emergencies, like Vicars in ditches.'

In a matter of seconds he attached the rope to the rear bumper of the car and then to the tractor. He was back on his seat in a brace of shakes and began to pull the Vicar's car backwards.

'Stop!' I shouted. 'The door!'

It was too late. There was an ominous crack as the door decided to stay where it was, in the close embrace of the bank. Father Whittaker was speechless and breathing with great difficulty.

In the meanwhile the farmer had stopped the tractor and shouted over his shoulder.

'Did you say something?'

'The door is coming away from the car,' I yelled.

'Why didn't you close it, Vicar?' enquired the farmer when he turned round.

I am convinced, on reflection, that had Father Whittaker been carrying a shotgun, he would have filled Islwyn Jenkins full of lead at that moment. Instead he slew him with a glance.

'The Vicar couldn't close the door because it was stuck in the bank,' I said, acting as interpreter for my silent employer.

Islwyn jumped down from the tractor, unperturbed. 'Well, we'll have to release it, won't we?'

Release it he did with a mighty heave. The door came away

with a squelch, attached to the car by the merest thread.

'Hold the door up,' he said to Charles, 'while I go and get some binder twine.'

He disappeared up the road.

'I'll come and help you, Charles.' I was about to scramble out from the back when the Vicar bellowed. 'Let him hold it himself. He got us into this mess.'

Suddenly there was a sound of a car in the distance. As it drew nearer, the sound indicated a refined aristocratic engine.

A Bentley purred its way into sight and came to a halt, its bonnet in close proximity to the tractor which was now blocking the entrance to the drive.

Sir David Jones-Williams (Bart.) dismounted. He was a large man in his seventies, dressed in expensive tweeds and with an expensively coloured complexion to match. The title was bestowed upon the family in the last century as a reward for converting a couple of pretty valleys into industrial eyesores.

'Good God, man,' he blasphemed, addressing the Vicar. 'What's happened here? Not driving under the influence, I trust?'

I put my head out of the car window.

'Sir David, this is the new Vicar of Pontywen.'

'You!' he exclaimed. 'No wonder the car is in the ditch.'

'Allow me to explain, Sir David.' Father Whittaker had gathered up the tattered shreds of his dignity. 'We were coming to pay you a courtesy visit and on the way I was giving my other curate his first driving lesson.'

'I think you had better give the one in the back a whole course of lessons before you start on this poor devil.'

Charles was presenting a pitiful sight, standing in a morass which was now around his ankles and holding up a car door which was getting heavier by the minute. He had the look of an injured spaniel.

'Sorry about the tractor, Sir David.' The welcome voice of Islwyn Jenkins cut short any further embarrassing conversation. 'Once I've tied up the car door with binder twine, I'll have it out of the way in no time. Perhaps you would move your car back, sir.'

While the Squire was reversing his Bentley, Islwyn tied the inside door handle to the passenger seat firmly enough to hold the door in place. In seconds the car was out of the ditch.

Sir David had been watching the rescue operation from the driving seat of his saloon.

'Well done, Jenkins,' said the Baronet. 'If you will move your tractor out of the way, the Vicar and his – er – staff can follow me down the drive.'

Charles joined me in the back seat, his shoes and the bottoms of his trousers plastered with evil smelling slime.

'I think I had better stay outside, Vicar. I don't fancy treading on expensive carpets with my feet like this.'

'In that case you had better get out and make your apologies to Sir David when we get to the house.' The Vicar's tone was sharp. 'And by the way, Secombe, what did he mean about you needing a course of driving lessons?'

'I'm afraid I was driving Canon Llewellyn's car last summer and we collided at the top of Church Street. He was on the wrong side of the road but swears that I was the culprit.'

Father Whittaker tutted.

When we reached the front of the mansion, which had been built in 1880 to resemble a grade three castle with all mod. cons., the Squire was standing in the doorway. He sported a white military moustache which gave him a formidable appearance.

'Come on in,' he barked. It was an order not a request.

'If you don't mind, Sir David,' stammered Charles, 'I think I had better stay outside because of my shoes.'

'Nonsense,' said the Squire. 'Give 'em a good old scraping on that,' there was a scraper at the side of the door, 'then a good wipe on the doormat and you'll be all right.'

While Charles was engaged in vigorous exercise on the scraper, Sir David indulged himself with an attempt at banter.

'Here endeth the first lesson, eh, young man?' He guffawed at his own joke.

We were shown into the drawing room. With its massive french windows overlooking the lawn, it was like the film sets I had seen from the one-and-nines in the Rialto in Swansea.

'Take a seat while I get Mrs Pengelly to make us some tea.'

Father Whittaker savoured the surroundings. It was obvious that Llanhyfryd Hall would be number one on his visiting list, with his next visit minus his entourage.

'This,' he said, 'is gracious living.'

Charles and I nodded.

Sir David returned to the drawing room.

'She'll have some tea for us in the dining room in half an hour or so. Well, Vicar, what do you think of Pontywen?'

Our employer blinked behind his big spectacles, put his head on one side, and paused, in an effort to look sagacious.

'To me it represents a challenge. I have yet to take its spiritual temperature. Very shortly we shall undertake a door-to-door survey after which I shall be better able to make an assessment and plan accordingly.

As an attempt to impress the old Squire, it was a total failure.

'I don't wish to hear about spiritual temperatures and plans. The last thing I want in the parish church is any alteration to the services. Canon Llewellyn's way of doing things was splendid and couldn't be bettered. What I meant was what do you think of the people and the town?'

Father Whittaker looked like a man who had just been given a nasty blow in the solar plexus.

'Oh, well – er – Sir David, from what I've seen so far, I – er – think the people seem warm hearted and – er – the town a nice place in which to live.'

From then on the conversation revolved around life in the countryside and what it had to offer compared with life in big cities. By the time we left, it was apparent that the Squire had dropped his animosity towards me and had transferred it to the Vicar.

As he stood outside the house to see us off, he ventured one more light hearted reference to the afternoon's happenings.

'What's that thing in the bible about ending up in the ditch?'

'"Can the blind lead the blind? Shall they not both fall into the ditch?"' I said, relishing every word.

'That's it,' replied the Squire. 'Jolly good.'

He guffawed again.

The Vicar glared at me.

As we were driving off, I received a reprimand. 'There was no need for you to supply the quotation.'

I told Mrs Richards that evening about our adventures and the Squire's words about not altering the services.

'Serves him right,' she said. 'Starting to talk about dressing up in those investments. Mind, perhaps I could put up with that but once he'd start doing that other thing, I'd never go to church again.'

'What's that, Mrs Richards?'

'Burning those insects.'

10

'I think it was divine intervention that impelled you into the ditch.' Charles and I, clad in our cassocks were on our way to the daily service the day after the happening.

'What do you mean?' said my fellow curate who was still shaken.

'It means, O thou who art slow of understanding, that Father will not be inflicting any more driving lessons upon you. Can you ride a bike?'

'Of course. I used to ride one when I was at university. I still have it at home.'

'In that case, suggest to our master this morning that you cycle to Llanhyfryd and then get your parents to send it by rail ready for Sunday.'

'Fred, you're a genius. One more lesson and I'd have a nervous breakdown.'

And so it was that Father Whittaker had his Austin Big Seven restored to its pristine condition never to entrust it to Charles's tender care again. At the same time he was able to 'anchor' him in the little church where he could do the least harm, to their mutual satisfaction.

On the Monday of the next week we were launched into our door-to-door survey. 'We shall pray for the five streets we shall visit this week,' said the Vicar at the daily service.

Later, at our meeting in the Vicarage, I asked him whether we had to visit only those who were not members of our churches.

'We visit everybody,' he said. 'I know Canon Llewellyn had his list but it was incomplete. Don't forget I want to have full details – age, baptised or confirmed. If they belong to other denominations I want to know what they are. If they are non believers, I want to know that.'

'Don't you think it is rather impolite to ask people their age?' I enquired.

'If they don't wish to give it, just estimate,' he replied. 'By the way, I shall not be with you this afternoon. I have a missionary meeting in Cardiff.'

As we left the Vicarage, each with a folder full of forms, I said to Charles, 'Thank heaven for the missionary meeting. At least we shall not be under his eagle eye. By the way, as far as I am concerned, everybody's age will be an estimate.'

'Me, too,' replied my colleague.

At two-thirty we met in Thomas Street.

'You take the right-hand side and I'll do the other side,' I suggested. 'Whoever finishes first will come and help the other one.'

'I expect you will be first,' forecast my colleague hopefully.

'Go to the ant, thou sluggard,' I said.

'What number is she?' he asked facetiously.

'Number one, Thomas Street.' I pointed to the first of the houses across the road. Holding his folder he approached the house with as much eagerness as a patient entering a dentist's surgery. He knocked on the door timidly.

'There's nobody in,' he shouted to me.

'Knock harder.'

This time he knocked harder.

A peroxide blonde, in her forties by the look of her, opened the door. The next minute Charles had been invited inside.

I knocked on the door of number two. Faltering footsteps down the passage heralded the approach of an old lady who opened the door a few inches.

'What is it?'

'We're doing a survey of the street. Can you tell me what denomination you are?'

'Labour and proud of it,' she answered and shut the door in my face.

I opened my folder.

'No. 2, Thomas Street,' I wrote. 'Name and age not divulged. Age estimated at 80. Non believer.'

Numbers four and six were answerless.

At number eight, the door was opened by a man in his thirties, with a couple of blue scars on his face indicating his mining profession. 'The wife's out,' he said.

'You'll do,' I answered. 'We're doing a survey of the street for the Church. Can you tell me, please, what denomination you are?'

'What do you mean?'

'Well, are you Church or Chapel?'

'Oh, I see. C. of E. 'ere.'

'May I have your name, please?'

'Wait a minute. What's going on 'ere? 'Oo are you?'

'I'm the Curate of Pontywen. My name is Fred Secombe. We have a new Vicar and he wants to find out how many families are Church families.'

'Oh, I see. My name is Phillips.'

'Married, Mr Phillips?'

'Yes.'

'Any children?'

'Five.'

'What ages are they?'

'Ten, eight, six, four and two.'

'Nicely spaced out, every two years, I see.'

'That's the way the wife wanted it.'

'Very methodical is she?'

'Yes, that's 'er ten-year plan, like Stalin.' He grinned.

'Has she got another plan?'

'No, that's enough, she said.'

'Now then, are you baptised?'

'No, I've been christened, though.'

'That's the same thing.'

'Is it? Well, would you believe it.'

'Is your wife baptised?'

'Yes. She's been done. At least, I think she 'as.'

'How about the children? Have they been baptised?'

'No. What 'appened was, we 'ad the first one a bit quick and before we could get around to it, then the next one was on 'is way. So we've 'ad no chance what with me on shift work, like. But one of these days we'll get round to it and 'ave 'em done together.'

'Thank you, Mr Phillips. You have been very helpful.'

The look of relief on his face as he closed the door was most touching.

There was no sign of Charles.

Number ten was Baptist. Number twelve was Welsh Methodist. Number fourteen was Pentecostal. The old lady at number sixteen when asked her denomination, said 'I listens to the wireless, love.' I decided to write that down on the form to indicate to the Vicar how irrelevant most of these answers were. It was becoming apparent to me that when asked their religious allegiance, the occupants would say any denomination but C. of E. to get me away from their doorsteps.

There was still no sign of Charles.

At number eighteen I was invited inside by an elderly man, bearing a number of blue scars and coughing intermittently.

'Sorry about the cough. It's the dust, Vicar. Forty years down the mines. The price of coal. Nothing in my pocket, only in my lungs. No, I 'aven't bothered about religion, to tell you the truth. A couple of times down below, I said a prayer when I was trapped by a fall. I suppose it must 'ave worked. I think 'e must 'ave owed it to me for putting up with the conditions down there. Would you like a cup of tea?'

'No, thank you very much. We have to get round all the houses in the street, you see.'

'Well, any time you want to pop in 'ere, you'll always be welcome.'

On my form, I put down his name, Edwin Jones, widower, and alongside the remark, 'Non believer. Lonely, sick. Needs a visit.'

Number twenty-two was 'C. of E. non attending' while number twenty-four housed a full blooded Communist. 'Edgar Matthews, non believer, Marxist,' was the entry on the form.

For a quarter of an hour on his doorstep he and I indulged in a verbal battle. It reminded me of an episode in the 1940 National Union of Students' Conference at Leeds University which I had attended as President of the Students' Union of my college.

I had gone down to the gents' cloakroom to collect my overcoat only to find a crowd of students gathered in a ring around two men. At first I thought it was a stand up fight. On joining the onlookers I discovered that they were being enthralled by a debate on the existence of God. The protagonist for God was an African student, and the defender of the Marxist faith was a north countryman.

For half an hour we were held spellbound by a brilliant interchange of argument. The African had all the apologetics for the existence of God at his finger tips whilst the Englishman was using the Marxist battering ram against them. At the end of the discussion both champions of their causes shook hands and called a truce. As the African said, quoting Sydney Smith, 'we are like two women slanging each other across a street. We can never agree because we are arguing from different premises.'

Here was I, on a much lower level, engaged in a similar activity in Pontywen. The last word came from Edgar. 'Why can't my wife wear a fur coat, the same as the wife of a capitalist, if as you say, we're all equal in the sight of God.'

Number twenty-six was the last of the houses on my side of the street. The lady of the house was a Jehovah's Witness and was intent on teaching me the meaning of the Bible as an Old Moore's Almanac. It took ten minutes and a certain amount of rudeness on my part to disentangle myself from this forceful female's attentions.

Still Charles was nowhere to be seen. I debated as to whether I should start on number twenty-five or go back to number one to see if my inept colleague was still incarcerated with the blonde. I decided on the latter course.

I gave the knocker a hearty thumping. A minute passed. Just as I was about to repeat the process, the door opened, 'Come on in,' said the blonde, 'and join your friend. We're just about to have another cup of tea.'

'If you don't mind, I'd rather not,' I replied, 'and I don't think my colleague should do so either. We have to complete a survey of this street by the end of the afternoon.'

With that, Charles emerged from the front room.

'I'm sorry, Mrs Williams. I didn't realise what the time was. I'm afraid I had better get on with my work.'

'"Get on with my work"!' I exploded. 'You've only just started and I have finished the whole of the other side of the street.'

'It's my fault,' said Mrs Williams. 'I've 'ad such an un'appy life with my 'usband and your friend 'ave been very sympathetic.'

'Glad to hear it,' I grunted.

'See you again, Mrs Williams,' were Charles's parting words.

'If you're a wise man you won't,' I warned him as she closed the door. 'Come into my parlour said the spider to the fly.'

'No, she's not like that. She said that he beats her up and doesn't give her enough money for food.'

'For somebody who gets beaten up and is underfed, she looks a picture of health and is well upholstered. Good heavens, Charles, grow up, will you?'

He dropped his head like a child who had just been scolded.

'Look, Charles. You get down to number twenty-five and work back towards me.'

He crawled down the street.

I knocked on the door of number three. A large unkempt lady who must have been in her fifties appeared.

'All right, Father, I'll go and get the money now,' she said.

'I'm not who you think I am,' I replied. 'I'm the curate from the parish church, Church of England. We are finding out people's denominations. I know what yours is now so I shan't waste any more of your time.'

'Oh, that's all right, love. Don't worry. Anyway, if ever you're collecting for anything, you can always come 'ere. I won't be able to give much but you can 'ave it with pleasure.'

Number five produced a thin, tiny little woman with bird-like features, neatly dressed.

'Yes?' she asked sharply.

I launched into my preamble once more.

'C. of E. 'ere. Always 'ave been.'

'Good. May I have your name, please.'

'Wilkins. Miss.'

'Are you baptised?'

'Certainly and confirmed, too. I've got my communion book still, signed by the Bishop.'

'I don't think I have seen you at Communion.'

'Perhaps I was there when you weren't there. 'Ave you been next door?' She pointed to number three.

'Yes. I've just called there.'

'She's terrible. Shouts, swears. Spoils the 'ole street. We like to keep ourselves to ourselves 'ere.'

'Christians are not supposed to keep themselves to themselves, Miss Wilkins. Jesus said that at the day of judgement, He will ask you what you have done for other people. If I were you I shouldn't tell Him you've kept yourself to yourself.'

'You're a cheeky young man,' she snapped and banged the door in my face.

Once again there was no sign of Charles but coming towards me was Will Book and Pencil.

'Just the man I want to see, Reverend.'

'It wasn't me, I swear, Constable.'

'Very funny, Mr Secombe, but I'm afraid it's on a serious matter.'

He has found out the origin of the Christmas tree in St Padarn's, I thought – not to mention the beer barrel.

'I've got to go to number fifteen, name of Harrington. The son has been playing truant from school and was knocked down this afternoon on the main road. He's up the hospital. They're afraid he might not live. He was conscious enough to give his name and address before he passed out.'

I was stunned. Barry Harrington was one of the choirboys in the parish church. A born mimic, he used to do a wicked impression of Canon Llewellyn singing the responses. Father Whittaker would be a gift to his talents.

'Do you mind coming with me?' asked the policeman.

'Of course not. I know the boy anyway. He's in the choir at the parish church.'

Barry's parents were well wishers rather than churchgoers. Mrs Harrington, a pleasant little lady, was very reserved and under the thumb of her six-foot tall husband who had a surface job at the colliery which had saved him from the forces.

The policeman knocked on the door with such force that the noise echoed round the street. There was a scurry of footsteps down the passage. Mrs Harrington's face lost every vestige of colour when she saw the policeman and the curate on her doorstep.

'There's been an accident at the pit...' Her hand clutched her breast.

'No, Mrs Harrington. Can we come in, please?' said Will gently.

We were shown into the front room where on the mantelpiece was a photograph of Barry in his choir robes.

'I'm afraid the accident has happened to your son – down on

109

the main road. He's in the hospital.'

Her eyes opened wide in disbelief.

'He's in school. He couldn't have been on the main road.'

I went and sat beside her on the settee. I put my arm round her shoulders.

'He must have been playing truant,' I said. 'It seems that he was in collision with a car.'

'Oh my God! Don't say that he's –' She couldn't bring herself to say the dreaded word.

'He's alive, Mrs Harrington,' the policeman assured her, 'but he's very ill.'

'If you get your coat and hat on, I'll walk up to the hospital with you. Perhaps the constable will get in touch with your husband at the colliery in the meanwhile.'

She accepted my offer to escort her and we were out of the door in no time. In the street there was still no sign of Charles.

As we walked, the mother talked in gasps about her one and only child.

'I can't understand why he should have "mitched" from school. He's no angel and he loves a bit of mischief now and again but to stay away from his class, that's not like him at all. Perhaps he was with another boy who led him astray. You know what some boys are like.'

The shock of the news caused this normally reserved little lady to chatter incessantly all the way to the hospital. She did not stop until we went into the side ward where Barry had been taken. The boy's head was swathed in bandages. An elderly doctor was at the bedside.

'I'm afraid your son has a suspected fractured skull and a fractured pelvis. The next few days will be critical. I'll leave you with him for a while until nurses come to attend to him. He's unconscious and probably will remain so for some time.'

He paused at the door.

'We are doing everything in our power, you can rest assured, Mrs Harrington.'

When he left, the mother sat on a chair by her son's bedside and smoothed his cheek. The flow of words had come to an end. I brought a chair from the corner and sat beside her.

'Would you like me to say a prayer?' I asked.

She nodded.

'Our Father . . .' I began. She joined me in the Lord's Prayer, whispering the words, as if afraid to disturb the boy's sleep.

I prayed for his recovery and that his parents would have strength to face the ordeal.

'Thank you,' she whispered.

She never uttered another word until her husband arrived half an hour later. A big, burly man he burst into tears as soon as he saw his son.

'Come on, Llew,' she said. 'We've got to pull ourselves together for Barry's sake.'

'They're doing all they can for him, Mr Harrington. All we can do is to pray for him.'

So saying I arose and led him to the chair alongside his wife.

'I shall be in touch and we shall be praying for him in church tomorrow morning.' With those words, I left the pair of them. She was comforting her husband and was still tearless.

As I left the hospital, I was praying hard that the outcome for Barry would not be like that for little David William.

I still carried the folder and the forms. I had an almost overwhelming urge to scatter them over the hillside as an irrelevance. Instead I walked back to Thomas Street to find out if my colleague had completed his stint. I had been away for more than an hour. Since I left him at number twenty-five, the end house, I decided to call at number seven where he should have made the last of his visits.

The lady of the house claimed to be Welsh Baptist and had not seen Charles. One by one I made my way down the street until I arrived at number twenty-five in a state of high dudgeon. My assault on the knocker made that of Will Book and Pencil sound like a mere tap.

Footsteps hurried down the passage. A pleasant faced lady, middle-aged and motherly, appeared. 'He's finishing his tea with my husband in the middle room. My husband's been having his dinner, being on six till two, and your friend had a little something with him. Methodist we are, but always pleased to see the clergy.'

I had no time to say anything because Charles Wentworth-Baxter loomed up behind her.

'I'd better be going now, Mrs Hopkins, and thank you for the tea. Ah, well, on with the work.'

Words failed me.

'Been nice meeting you, Mr Wedgewood-Baxter,' she said and closed the door.

'"On with the work"!' I expostulated. '"On with the work"! I have trudged around twenty-four houses, escorted a lady to the hospital to see her badly injured son, and in that time you have called at two houses! Let me tell you, Charles, you will be having the boot if you do this when Father is with us.'

'But, Fred, they were such nice people.'

'I expect Pontywen is full of such nice people but if we are going to carry on with this stupid exercise, you'll have to pull your finger out, I tell you.'

I turned on my heels and marched back to number thirteen, Mount Pleasant View, still seething.

'You've got a face like a thunderstorm,' commented Mrs Richards.

'It's that idiot, Charles. His trouble is that he is a lazy good-for-nothing. I visited twenty-four houses this afternoon while he managed two. Not only that, I spent an hour in between taking Mrs Harrington to the hospital where Barry is critically ill after an accident on the main road.'

'Oh dear,' said my landlady. 'It's that little boy in the choir, the one who's always making the other boys in stitches.'

'I'm afraid he's the one in stitches now, Mrs Richards. It looks very serious to me. I think I'd better let the vicar know after tea. After all the boy is in his anchorage at the parish church.'

By seven o'clock I felt sufficiently calm to make the journey to the Vicarage.

Father Whittaker opened the door and when he saw me his face developed one of Mrs Richards' 'thunderstorms'.

'The man I want to see,' he said, through his clenched dentures. 'Come on in.'

'You want to follow St James' advice and keep control of your tongue.'

I followed this advice and managed to control my tongue, confining it to a simple question.

'What do you mean, Vicar?'

'I've just had a lady here from Thomas Street who claimed that you abused her verbally this afternoon.'

112

'Excuse me, Vicar,' I was fighting hard to keep control, 'that lady verbally abused her Roman Catholic next-door neighbour who was concerned to help my cause, and then she went on to suggest that the great thing in life was to keep yourself to yourself. I told her she should follow the advice of Jesus to do the opposite. I'm sure St James would have done the same.'

His mouth opened but no words came forth, as if he were struck dumb.

'In any case, I have come here on a matter much more serious than Miss Wilkins' ruffled feelings. One of your choir boys, Barry Harrington, was knocked over on the main road this afternoon and is fighting for his life in the hospital.'

Father Whittaker stood up.

'What ward is he in?'

'Ward seven. I expect his mother and father will be with him. I took Mrs Harrington there this afternoon and I've said prayers with him.'

'Thank you,' he said. 'I'll go now to see them. We'll – er – discuss Miss Wilkins some other time.'

With those words, he was out through the door and then drove up the drive like Jehu, leaving a greatly impressed curate on the doorstep.

11

'It's your turn now,' said Aneurin the MD. 'Look at them. They're like a bunch of excited children and I'm not just referring to my pupils. Some of these mature men seem to have gone back to early childhood.'

He and I were standing at the piano, surveying the scene as an eager band of helpers directed by Sergeant Major Bertie Owen cleared away chairs at the back of St Padarn's to make floor space. The time for the first stage rehearsal had arrived. For three months the chorus had been drilled in the music of *The Pirates of Penzance*. Now they had to be transformed into pirates, policemen and twelve daughters of Major-General Stanley.

As I looked at Bertie Owen prancing about the floor, my heart sank. He was difficult to control while he was sitting on a chair doing his best to murder the music. On his two feet in rehearsals he would be a menace.

Clutching my brand-new prompt copy of the opera purchased from Bridget D'Oyly Carte out of my hard-earned stipend, I called for order.

'Just as Aneurin has demanded discipline in the music rehearsals, I shall expect the same from you on stage. I don't want any fooling around. As you know I have brought you all together for this evening. This is simply to give you a taste of what is involved in the production. As from next week, there will be sectional rehearsals.'

'What do you mean by that?' enquired Bertie.

'It means, for example, that next week and the week after we shall be doing Act One. In that case there is no point in having the police here who are only in Act Two. Occasionally I shall only have the girls here and, more often, men only. So this evening, we shall have the opening chorus of Act One with the pirates and Samuel's solo. Then we shall have the entrance of the Major-General's daughters with the solo from Mabel, if she's here. We'll switch to Act Two for the entry of the police and finally we'll go back to Act One for the capture of the girls by the pirates. Now then, everybody off the floor except the pirates.'

The girls and the men playing the policemen went to the back, chattering like a crowd of ten-year-olds released into the school playground.

'Quiet!' I shouted. 'For heaven's sake let's have silence from those not involved in the action.'

I proceeded to group the nine men who were pirates. According to the D'Oyly Carte book there should have been eighteen pirates to eighteen girls. However, as the Pontywen Grammar School hall, booked for our performances via Aneurin, had a stage which could not accommodate a cast that size, it was just as well that male members were below par.

'Now then, before the curtain rises, there is the noise of merriment and some laughter which gets louder until when the curtain does go up on the fifteenth bar there's a cheer as Samuel comes on with a flagon of wine. He goes around starting on the right, filling cups, then goes to centre for the solo. In the second verse he goes left doing the same, and then back to centre. We'll do your little dance, Iorwerth, at a principals rehearsal.'

Iorwerth, the tenor, had been harbouring a strong desire to play Frederick, the romantic lead. As I was not only producer but also casting committee rolled into one, I had chosen myself to play Frederick since the female romantic lead was to be played by Eleanor. By suggesting that he understudied me, I had sweetened the bitter pill somewhat.

'Can we have the opening bars, Charles?'

There was no response. When I looked round, I found him engaged in earnest conversation with one of the more nubile of Aneurin's pupils.

'Charles,' I said sharply.

He almost fell off his chair.

'Sorry – What was that?'

'Can we have the opening bars, please?'

Aneurin tapped his music stand and started to conduct.

A faint murmur was heard from the pirates.

'Stop! Stop!' I shouted. 'Let's have some realism. You're a bunch of pirates getting merry on sherry, like the crowd in the Red Lion half an hour before closing time. Let's start again.'

Once again Charles began to play.

'Rhubarb, rhubarb. Ha! Ha! Ha! Rhubarb.' Bertie Owen was giving a solo performance at the top of his voice, watched in amazement by his fellow pirates.

I went over to Bertie, caught him by the shoulders and motioned to Aneurin to stop Charles who was intent on his piano playing.

'Rhubarb grows in gardens, Bertie. I asked you to be realistic not horticultural.'

'Excuse me, Mr Secombe. I always thought that everybody in crowd scenes says rhubarb all the time.'

'Somebody's been pulling your leg. So please never keep repeating the word rhubarb. Talk about anything you like and by the way, when you laugh, sound as if you're enjoying a joke, not forcing it like rhubarb. Once again, shall we start and don't forget that this is for the third time of asking.'

'Do I enter right centre or from the back, Mr Secombe?' Iorwerth was showing off, as a past performer amongst a bunch of novices.

'Right centre, Iorwerth. There'll be a rostrum so that you dominate the scene on your entrance.'

His chest expanded several inches.

'OK, Aneurin. Straight through this time. Don't forget plenty of life but no rhubarb.'

This time the chorus displayed signs of life and Bertie was too chastened to make himself the focus of attention. In any case, Iorwerth was determined to occupy that position and was so intent on posing on the rostrum that he almost forgot to move down to pour out his sherry.

'Iorwerth,' I said at the end of the chorus, 'When you sing "Strong his arm", you don't have to stop pouring and feel your muscles instead.'

'I thought it would help it come alive, Mr Secombe.'

'Let the words speak for themselves, Iorwerth. Your diction is excellent and doesn't need reinforcement.'

'Of course, thank you.'

Aneurin butted in.

'Chorus, can we have better diction from you? For example "Fred'ric's out of his indentures". Let's hear the "in". It sounds like Frederick's out of his dentures, the way you're singing it.'

'Right. Here we go again. Chorus, much better this last time but remember Aneurin's warning about diction.'

Apart from the fact that Iorwerth was so concerned with being larger than life that he forgot his words, the opening chorus showed signs of promise.

As the last notes died away, Eleanor entered at the back of the hall.

'We'll have a change of face now. Gentlemen, you can give place to the ladies. It's their turn to occupy the stage.'

The men shambled off the floor space and I went down to meet Eleanor.

'I'm shattered,' she said. 'I've just spent two hours delivering a very reluctant baby.'

'You poor thing. Do you think you'll be up to singing "Poor Wandering One"?'

'It won't be brilliant but I'll do my best.'

By now the girls were in a fever of excitement, as noisy as a flock of starlings settling in the branches of a tree.

'Calm down, girls. You are the Major-General's daughters not a crowd of factory workers on an outing to Barry Island. You are all terribly pukka, out for the afternoon with a stretch of sand for your private enjoyment. Some of you will have parasols and all of you will be walking very daintily on your toes, to avoid damp patches in the sand. You will be moving about in twos and threes and once you begin to sing come into two lines. There are dance steps you will learn at a later rehearsal. Just get the feel of things this evening.'

It took quite a while to sort out the groupings, sopranos together, altos together, with the prettier ones in the front and the not so pretty ones at the back.

Charles launched into the music.

'On your toes. Look happy. Smile. Show your teeth. Now then into the lines in which I arranged you. Don't bunch, spread yourselves out.'

Suddenly I was aware of Eleanor standing behind me.

'You're bawling at them like a tin-pot dictator. Show them what you want, how to walk, et cetera.'

'Stop, Stop!' I commanded. Everything ground to a halt, except the piano where Charles was caught up in the music. Aneurin tapped him on the shoulder with his baton. My colleague turned round, startled.

'You haven't stopped again,' he said, in exasperation.

'I have and I shall be stopping several times until we get everything right. OK Charles? Now then girls, Dr Davies will show you how to walk.'

She gave me a long hard look.

'For the purpose of this production, shall we drop the Doctor in front of my name! I'm Eleanor. I had not intended to become part of the production team. However since I have been hijacked into it, here goes. Get off the stage and then watch me.'

For the next five minutes or so in front of an intent audience she gave a lesson in movement worthy of a D'Oyly Carte production. She minced, she tripped along, she gave little gasps of surprise at something apparently discovered in a rock pool. All the time her mobile face indicated pleasure and delight at a seaside outing. I was proud of her.

'Now then, Mr Secombe, they're all yours.'

'Thank you very much. Girls, you couldn't have had a better illustration of what's required from you than that. So shall we start again.'

What followed was a complete transformation. Most of the girls were between sixteen and eighteen years of age with a few older ones in their twenties. They looked like daughters of the Major-General, young and fresh, and now they were beginning to move like them. The last time I had seen a production of *The Pirates of Penzance* the daughters looked more like his sisters.

Eleanor's solo was received with rapturous applause by the company.

'That was just like listening to Jenny Lind,' said Bertie to me.

'You've never heard Jenny Lind, Bertie. She was dead long before you were born.'

'Yes, but they called her a nightingale and that's how Dr Davies sounded.'

There was no answer to that.

'We'll have a break now,' I announced.

'I'm gasping for a cup of tea, Frederick.' Eleanor was sprawled across a chair. 'Why don't you get some of your ladies from the church to supply refreshments?'

'Very good idea. I think I'll ask Mrs Richards to get a couple of her friends to come along and do that. You must be tired out.'

'You can say that again. If you don't mind, I think I had better go now. I'll pick you up tomorrow evening at seven, if that's OK with you.'

I went to the door to see her off. She gave me a chaste salute on the doorstep and was away in her chariot in no time.

'How do you think it's shaping?' I asked Aneurin.

'I know it's very early days yet, but I think you've got a winner on your hands.'

'Coming from you, sir, that's very encouraging.'

'Time will tell,' said Aneurin.

'Shall we have the police, and the girls,' I shouted.

Idris the Milk who was playing the sergeant, had been hiding away in a corner, poring over his copy of the score. He looked terrified as he approached me.

'Look, Mr Secombe. I don't know whether I can do this. Can I bring my book on with me?'

'Idris, we have been through your solo several times. If you forget the words like Iorwerth, I'll shout them out to you. We are only going to do the entrance of the police, to get the hang of marching on stage and we'll stop after your first verse. We have to do that because Mabel's had to go home after delivering a baby.'

His face broke into a large grin.

'OK. I'll 'ave a go anyway.'

I grouped the girls around the floor space and put the men into line with Idris at their head.

'The kind of march I want from you men is a sort of Charlie Chaplin walk but not too exaggerated.'

I strutted around the floor, using Aneurin's baton as a truncheon.

'Just pretend you have a truncheon this evening. When we have the next rehearsal for the police, I'd like you to bring a stick of some kind with you. March around the stage once then form into a line behind the sergeant who is in the centre. Shall we go then?'

Idris, whose flat feet had secured him exemption from military service, was a natural for the part of the sergeant. He led off in splendid style, followed by eight policemen who varied from the introvert to the extrovert. It took half a dozen attempts before the entrance took shape.

'Back to Act One for the capture of the girls by the pirates and then we finish for the evening.'

I positioned the girls around the floor.

'Now then, men, you creep up behind the girls ready to catch them as they turn. They struggle with you then drop on their knees facing you.'

It was obvious that this was going to be the highlight of the evening. The men who were pirates, most of them middle-aged, relished the prospect of grabbing hold of the girls. Those who were police began to feel that they were miscast. The girls became giggly as they contemplated the action involving men.

In the middle of the noisy excitement which followed my words, Will Protheroe, a man in his sixties, tenor and pirate, came up to me.

'I'm sorry, Mr Secombe, but I'll 'ave to back out of this.'

'What do you mean, Will?'

'It's my missis. She'll kill me if she sees me catching 'old of them young girls. She'll never speak to me again.'

'But it's only play acting.'

'She won't understand that. I'll tell you what. I'll come and sing behind the scenes if you like. As for going in front of people and doing that, you can count me out.'

If only Bertie Owen had a wife like that, I thought, it would be much easier to direct the opera. As it was, he was acting like a teenager pretending to struggle with two sixteen-year-olds. On the other hand, Will Protheroe's strategic withdrawal would result in a neat mathematical equation of two girls each to one man.

'Quiet!' My stentorian exercise produced an instant silence.

'It will have to be two girls to each man. The men will grab a girl's waist in each hand and there will be a short struggle. I mean short, not an all-in wrestling bout. The girls drop on their knees facing the pirate after singing "too late" for the second time. You stay there, girls, till you rise facing front to sing "We have missed our opportunity of escaping with impunity".'

It was too much to expect Bertie to remain subdued for long. While the rest of the men crept up quickly behind the girls he decided on a flying tackle. The two girls and himself landed on the floor in a giggling heap.

'Bertie, for heaven's sake, this is not a rugby match. If it was, you wouldn't be so keen on the tackle. You creep up and grab their waists, not bowl them over. Can we start again, please?'

By now the rest of the men were getting tired of Bertie's antics and were making it plain. Iorwerth put it succinctly, 'Bertie, you're acting like a bloody two-year-old.' This had the desired effect and for twenty minutes a good time was had by all except the police who looked on, glum faced at missing the *pièce de résistance*.

'Next week,' I announced. 'Act One. Principals rehearsal next Sunday evening after church at eight p.m.'

Charles came up to me.

'Do you think the Vicar will allow that? After all it is Lent.'

'What the eye doesn't see, the heart doesn't grieve, Charles. There's no need for him to know. In any case, as you told me before Christmas, I am in charge of St Padarn's.'

He looked crestfallen.

Idris the Milk lingered after the crowd had made their way out.

'Do you fancy some fish and chips since you are on your own?'

'I'd love some,' I said. 'Bertie, would you mind seeing to everything.'

He came up to me, looking very sheepish.'Sorry about tonight. Once I get the hang of things, I'll be fine, you see. You go now, I'll lock up.'

'Poor old Bertie,' said Idris, as we made our way to the fish and chip shop, 'if only 'is 'ead was as good as 'is 'eart 'e'd be great.'

Soon Idris and I were sitting on either side of a blazing fire while Gwen was cutting bread and butter to go with the fish and chips warming in the oven.

'How did it go?' she asked.

'Very well for a first rehearsal. I think your husband is going

121

to be an excellent Sergeant of Police.'

'Look out, Will Book and Pencil. Your job's no longer safe,' she quipped. 'Our Percy wants to come and watch one night, if that's all right with you.'

'Of course, with pleasure. Wait a moment. It wouldn't be a bad idea if he joined the police.'

'What do you mean?'

'Well, in most productions of *Pirates* there is always a little policeman on the end. Percy can be that little man.'

'Oh, he'd be thrilled, wouldn't he, Idris?'

Idris was not so enthusiastic.

'What about 'omework and being out late at night?'

'He could do his homework before he came,' said Gwen.

'In any case, I'd only need him at a few rehearsals, and he needn't stay to the end.'

'Righto, on those conditions, fine.'

Halfway through our fish and chips, Gwen dropped a bomb-shell.

'I hear that Elspeth Evans is going out with Mr Wentworth-Baxter.'

Elspeth was the sixteen-year-old member of the chorus who distracted Charles's attention at the beginning of the rehearsal that evening. She was a well developed young lady, blonde haired and blue eyed, who looked older than her years.

'Where did you get that from, Gwen?'

'Our next-door neighbour saw them together last Sunday evening at the back of the cemetery.'

The back of the cemetery was a haven for courting couples in the dark winter evenings.

'So that's why he was not enthusiastic about Sunday night rehearsals. I wondered why he had become conscious of the season of Lent.'

'I thought you ought to know. The family haven't got a very good name and Mr Wentworth-Baxter is a bit – er – easily led. Believe me, Elspeth will lead him up the garden path, if anybody will. She's got quite a reputation.'

For the past few weeks I had not seen so much of Charles. Now the reason was plain. Curates were warned at theological college of the inadvisability of consorting with young ladies who lived in the parish. A sixteen-year-old schoolgirl came into the category of strictly forbidden. He had something to hide even from me.

It seemed that my colleague was hell bent on self destruction. Already the new Vicar had warned him about his habit of arriving late for services at Llanhyfryd – an offence which was aggravated by the way in which he conducted the service. Constantly he was announcing the wrong hymns and once forgot that he had not administered the bread to a second row of communicants and simply presented them with the chalice. Worst of all for his countryside congregation was the abstruse nature of his sermons. They could not understand a word of what he was saying.

He was an up-to-date version of a cartoon which appeared in *Punch* in the last century. It showed the parson in the pulpit addressing a handful of country bumpkins, with straw in their hair. 'As you all know from your Aristotle', was the caption.

If the Vicar discovered that Charles was walking out with a schoolgirl, his stay in Pontywen would be terminated forthwith. I decided to talk the matter over with Eleanor the following night. All these thoughts were going through my head as I walked back to my digs.

There was a light in my front room. It was long past Mrs Richards' bed time. I opened the front door and was confronted by Charles who had come out of the room on hearing my key in the lock. He was in a state of great excitement.

'I've got something to tell you.'

'Let me get my coat off first, please. Go back to the room and I'll be with you now.'

No sooner had I divested myself and entered my sanctum, than he rushed up to me.

'You have been my best friend and you must be the first to know.'

'Know what, Charles?'

'I've got engaged.'

12

It was one o'clock in the morning when Charles left the house. For two hours I had tried all kinds of arguments to show him the folly of his ways.

'Charles, a sixteen-year-old schoolgirl, living in a council house and you an impecunious Curate. What sort of recipe is that for a successful marriage?'

'Elspeth says we can live with her parents until we find rooms somewhere.'

'Has she asked her parents about this?'

'No, I've told her to keep it a secret for the time being. I haven't given her a ring yet.'

'Can you imagine a schoolgirl keeping a secret like that from her school friends?'

'She's very grown up in many ways. I'm sure she can.'

'Yes, I've heard she's very grown up and in some of the less desirable connotations of the term.'

'What do you mean by that?'

'In other words, she has something of a reputation.'

He turned scarlet with anger not embarrassment.

'Who told you that?' he shouted.

'Keep your voice down, please. You'll be waking Mrs Richards in a minute. I shan't tell you who told me. All I shall say is that it was somebody very reliable.'

'I don't care who told you. It's a lie. She's not like that.'

We went over the same ground several times. However, by the time he left, I had made him promise not to say anything to the Vicar at the moment.

When I called for Charles on my way to morning service, I

found him in a state of semi-torpor. Our midnight discussion had left its mark on him.

'The rehearsal last night seems to have exhausted Charles,' said Myfanwy Howells, his landlady, when she opened the door to me. She had been recruited to play the part of Ruth, the Pirate Maid of all work. 'In any case he's been out late quite a few nights over the past weeks and it must catch up on him some time.'

He crawled out from his room to meet me and scowled in silence all the way to the parish church.

'For someone who has got engaged the night before, you don't appear to be over the moon,' I said to him at the church gates.

'And whose fault is that?' he replied, glaring at me.

Mattins was its usual uneventful self until it came to the second lesson read by the Vicar. It was from the thirteenth chapter of St Matthew's Gospel, the parable of the wheat and the tares.

'"The servants of the householder came and said to him, Sir, didst thou not sow good seed in thy field? From whence then hath it tares?

'"He said unto them, an enema hath done this."'

I was seized with a fit of coughing. The Vicar halted in his tracks and looked at me solicitously, evidently fearing for my health. Charles remained in his zombie state, his mind occupied with the back of the cemetery and the charms of Elspeth Evans.

'That was a nasty fit of coughing,' said Father Whittaker after the service.

'I get them occasionally,' I replied. 'It's an uncontrollable frog in my throat.'

'Try Fisherman's Friends. They'll get rid of the frog,' he advised. 'By the way, Fred, I'd like to see you in the Vicarage. Wentworth-Baxter, I'll see you at the top end of Mafeking Street at two-thirty prompt.'

Charles shambled out of the vestry, only too glad to be free for the rest of the morning and to recover some of his lost sleep.

The street visiting was going apace, and over half the parish was covered. With the Vicar cracking the whip, Charles had increased his work rate from the initial two houses to at least ten in an afternoon.

In the few weeks since the Barry Harrington episode the Vicar had become more friendly towards me, especially since he had learned that Doctor Eleanor Davies and I were not far off announcing our engagement. Such was my prestige that he addressed me by my Christian name nowadays whereas Charles was still in his double barrelled surname state. 'Class distinction,' said my colleague.

'An up-date on young Barry Harrington,' said the Vicar, while we were having coffee. 'He came out of the coma yesterday and they think his brain will not be affected but his fractured pelvis will keep him in hospital for six months, to say the least.'

Whatever faults my superior had, and they were many, I had to admire his pastoral zeal. There were very few days when he was not at the boy's bedside.

'Now then, Fred. I wonder if you'd mind taking my place at the Deanery missionary meeting this afternoon. As you know, I was at the Diocesan meeting a month ago and I feel that I should be pressing on with our parish survey instead of spending another couple of hours going over the same ground. The service is in Abermadoc parish church at three p.m. followed by a meeting in the back room of the Bull Inn where we have our Chapter meeting, as you know. The preacher is Canon William Parry.'

I could scarce contain my glee at this request. First, it would be a reprieve from the tedium of the parish survey. Second, it would be an opportunity to hear the Canon, whose pulpit oratory was a byword amongst the junior clergy. Apparently he had an amusing habit of exaggerating the consonants at the end of each word. It was said that at every committal in the burial service, he would say 'ashesum to ashesum, duster to duster'.

The bus dumped me at the Bull Inn at a quarter to three. As I left the vehicle, its solitary passenger for the last stage of the journey, the Rural Dean's car pulled into the Inn's car park. The last time I had seen him was when he visited my lodgings to pass on the request from Llanhyfryd that I should walk the four miles to service on Sundays.

To mark the occasion of a service with a visiting preacher, The Reverend Daniel Thomas BA, Rural Dean, had decided to wear spats, fawn in colour. He unfolded himself from his small car and was locking the door as I approached.

'Ah, Mr Seagrove, nice to see you. Where's your Vicar?'

'He has asked to be excused, Mr Rural Dean. He is very busy with the parish survey.'

'With the what?' The old man looked at me, bewildered.

'The Vicar is visiting every house in Pontywen and making a list of their denominations and names et cetera.'

'Well, well. Fancy that. What is he going to do when he's found out everything?'

'He hasn't decided yet.'

'Well, well. I hope he hasn't wasted his time. Good afternoon, Mrs Matthews.'

The Rural Dean took off his hat to the landlady who was standing in the doorway of the pub. As he did so, her Yorkshire terrier came up behind him and lifted his leg over the spotlessly clean spats. A stream of dark brown liquid anointed the virgin territory.

Mrs Matthews looked at me with a silent plea to say nothing. I looked up to the heavens, shrugged my shoulders and raised my hands – the conspiracy to keep mum was agreed.

Into the vestry of Abermadoc parish church went the dignitary with his case of robes and his discoloured spats. I retired to the privacy of the nature reserve-cum-churchyard to indulge in private mirth.

When I entered the old Saxon, plus Norman, plus Victorian church ten minutes later there were some twenty souls in the congregation: ten ladies and ten clerics. An elderly lady in tweeds was pedalling away at the organ, attempting a version of Handel's 'Largo'. The centuries-old musty smell conveyed an aura of antiquity to even the most insensitive of nostrils. Time had been petrified in St Mary's Abermadoc. The women whispered to each other, while the clergy had no inhibitions and indulged in ecclesiastical gossip double forte, 'too much at ease in Sion' as the Bishop once described such conduct.

Suddenly there was a loud cough from the back of the church, evidently a prearranged signal for the organist who threw up her hands in the air, only too pleased to be rescued from the intricacies of Handel. The Reverend Arthur Powell, Vicar of Abermadoc, intoned a vestry prayer using his nasal organ more than his vocal cords. One by one the congregation rose to their feet and the clerical procession of three ambled down the aisle, with the preacher and the Rural Dean in tandem at the front.

'Hymn number three fifty-eight. The three hundred and fifty-eighth hymn. Three five eight,' announced the Vicar. The organist began to play, only to be interrupted by the parson who read out the first line, 'From Greenland's icy mountains to India's coral strands'. There was a long pause in which she stared at the Vicar to make sure he was not going to read out the whole verse. He glared at her and waved an imperious hand. We launched into the missionary hymn, a few of the clergy bellowing the words while the rest, the very elderly, mouthed soundlessly. One of the ladies possessed a strong soprano voice. The other nine were content to allow her a solo virtuoso performance.

Arthur Powell, a man in his middle sixties, big, bull-necked and with a broken nose, looked more like a veteran boxer than a parson. It was only recently that he had come from a mining parish to spend the rest of his working days in the countryside. He read the first lesson from Isaiah, finishing strongly on the last verse 'For the nations kingdoms that will not serve thee shall perish.' He lingered lovingly on the word 'perish'. It was enough to frighten any non co-operative nation into the path of righteousness.

Evidently it frightened the organist to such an extent that she forgot that it is impossible to play a double chant to a psalm or canticle of nine verses without repeating the second half of the chant. The result was that the unsuspecting congregation was confronted with the latter part of the Gloria at the end of the Magnificat, while attempting to sing the first part of the chant. The organist, discovering too late what she had done, removed her hands from the keyboard. As the organ became silent, one by one the singers discovered what had happened and surrendered to the inevitable with uncertain notes hanging in the air. The congregation sat down in ones and twos, as if in a daze. I was only too thankful that it was the Rural Dean who had to read the second lesson and not myself.

By the time the preacher arrived in the pulpit I was prepared to make a quick exit from my seat in the back whenever it was necessary. 'The Second-er Book-er of Kings-um, the fifth-um chapter-um, first-er versum,' said the Canon. 'Now Naaman-er was a great-er man-er, but-er . . .' He repeated the text. Then he repeated the word 'but-er'.

Then followed a dramatic pause during which he stared at the congregation. He leaned over the edge of the pulpit, pointed his finger at them and whispered, 'He was a leper-um.' He repeated the words, this time in a booming voice and very slowly, 'He – was – a – leper-um.'

Canon Parry went on to explain that as chairman of the Diocesan missionary committee, he was standing in for a missionary who worked in the leper colonies of Africa. Several times in between long extracts from medical papers on the causes and effects of leprosy, he would stop and say, 'he was a leper-um.'

Eventually I decided I could not stay in my pew without disgracing myself. I slipped out through the back door into the pleasant March sunshine. I amused myself by reading the inscriptions on the tombstones which varied from the glorification of the departed to downright warnings to the non-departed. One message on a stone near the entrance to the churchyard was positively alarming. 'When this you see, pray think of me, what death to me hath done, and take great pains to be prepared, for death will surely come.'

It was more than half an hour later that the organ began to play for the last hymn. I crept into the back of the church hoping my absence had not been noticed. The Vicar gave us a nasal blessing and the service was over. A bemused congregation trooped out, punch drunk after the verbal battering from the Canon.

I joined the Reverend Amos Morris, a tall thin bespectacled man with a slight stoop. He was the Chapter Clerk (the secretary) of the Deanery. In his late fifties, he was the youngest man present, apart from myself.

'Pity the missionary couldn't come,' he drawled. He gave the impression that any slight exertion, including uttering a few sentences, would exhaust his strength. 'I've read that sermon before, except for the medical bits he put in out of some medical dictionary he must have got hold of.' He stopped and took a breath. 'It's out of a book of sermons I've got called *A Treasury of Pulpit Gems*.'

'It's a pity it wasn't like another pulpit gem I read about when I was in college,' I said.

'Which one was that?'

'A famous preacher at the end of the last century was billed to preach at evensong in All Saints, Margaret Street, on Easter Day. The church was packed and when the great man got into the pulpit, you could hear a pin drop. He waited a while and then shouted "Alleluia" and came down.'

'Very droll,' commented the Chapter Clerk. 'Would you like to collect the money for the tea and biscuits? It will save me the job.'

'With pleasure, Vicar.'

'In that case, I shall inform the Rural Dean.' With this last sentence he terminated the conversation and conserved his energy for the task of queuing for his cup of tea and a biscuit.

The back room of the Bull Inn which served as a meeting place for the Deanery clergy six times a year was redolent with stale tobacco and beer smells competing with that of furniture polish which came a poor third.

Mrs Matthews, the landlady, was at a table, pouring out tea. A plate of Marie biscuits was alongside the teacups and saucers. 'One biscuit each,' she announced.

On another table were some missionary pamphlets and a few books. Here the Reverend Williams-Ellis was in charge. It was he who made the trip to Cardiff once a year to purchase a study book for the chapter clergy. A thin, red-faced, buck-toothed man, in his late sixties, he looked around his potential customers as if he were a frightened rabbit surrounded by a pack of hounds. There was a run on the pamphlets but the books seemed destined to be returned to Cardiff in the Reverend Williams-Ellis's case.

Canon William Parry, a bald-headed, pink-faced man with rimless spectacles was in earnest conversation with the Rural Dean. Since I had no idea how much I had to ask for the tea and biscuits and with what receptacle I had to collect the money, I ventured to approach the two dignitaries.

'Excuse me, Mr Rural Dean,' I said, 'but how much am I to ask for the tea and biscuits and with what am I to collect it?'

'Hold on, young man,' he replied. 'I'll make the announcement now after I've thanked the Canon. It's threepence each and you can collect it on that what-you-call.' He pointed at a tea tray and then banged on the tray with a tea spoon. The conversation died away.

'I'm sure you'll all want me to thank Canon Parry for his splendid sermon about our brothers and sisters in Africa and all they've got to go through. Now then, Mr Seabourne will come round to collect threepence each for the tea and biscuits. Oh, and I forgot, we must thank Mr Powell for the use of his church.'

The Reverend Arthur Powell seized his opportunity.

'It's a pleasure, Mr Rural Dean. My only regret is that I could not invite you to a church hall instead of the back room of a pub. Perhaps in the fullness of time we shall be able to do so.'

How he was going to achieve this objective in a parish with a population of four hundred and a congregation of twenty he did not specify. All he had succeeded in doing was to alienate Mrs Matthews the landlady who looked like thunder.

As I went around collecting the threepences, I overheard the landlady say to one of the women, 'That's the last time they come here.'

It was at this point that the Rural Dean abandoned his habit of sitting on the fence. This time the iron had entered his soul. He could see the cosiness of his armchair by The Bull fireside being exchanged for an uncomfortable chair in a draughty church hall.

Once again he used his teaspoon, banging it on the side of his teacup with such force that it must have cracked it.

'There's one other person to thank and that is Mrs Matthews.' The clouds passed from the landlady's face, and landed on the Reverend Arthur Powell's countenance. 'We have been coming here to The Bull for our Deanery Chapter meetings for the past twenty years at least and I hope we shall be able to do so for the next twenty years.' As I looked at the clergy present, I estimated that at least three of them would have passed the century mark long before the next twenty years were up.

'We have always been very comfortable here and been made very welcome. Thank you, Mrs Matthews.'

The new Vicar of Abermadoc had a murderous expression on his face which went well with his broken nose. He resented losing on a technical knockout to a little bantam weight like the Rural Dean. As someone occupying a ringside seat, I felt like applauding the winner.

All the way back to Pontywen the rickety bus bounced its way over the decrepit road surfaces, churning my stomach in the process. Just before the bus pulled into the terminus at

Pontywen, I glanced out of the window and caught sight of two youngsters sitting and canoodling on a wall. It was the girl's blonde hair which attracted my attention. A closer look confirmed that it was Charles's beloved Elspeth.

'My word,' said Mrs Richards when she saw me. 'Your face is like a ghost.'

'It was the bus ride. I can't stand travelling in a bus any time but that journey was more like being on a switchback in a fairground.' I could not tell her that another reason for my pallor was the excitement at finding what should be the *coup de grâce* for my colleague's relationship with the schoolgirl.

'Those old buses always give my stomach the golly wobbles, too. They're too antique, that's the trouble.'

It was eight o'clock when the familiar sound of Eleanor's old Morris Minor disturbed the peace of Mount Pleasant View. A minute later there was a gentle tap on my window. When I opened the door, a somewhat damp fiancée presented herself.

'Permission to come in, sir, before I get drowned.'

I removed her raincoat which she had placed over her shoulders to make the few yards from the car to the doorstep. The rain was coming down in torrents.

'It's not a night for country lanes, Frederick.'

Our relationship had reached the stage when it was public property in Pontywen. That the curate and the lady doctor were courting was a topic which was now stale gossip. So we could spend the evening in my room, with the car parked outside, without causing any raised eyebrows in the street.

'A cup of tea before we settle down?'

'Yes, please. You sound as if we were bedding down for the night.'

'I don't mind if I do, sir,' I said, quoting the drunken Colonel Chinstrap in Tommy Handley's *ITMA*.

'Neither would I, but I'm afraid we shall have to wait for another year or so.'

'How long is the "or so"?'

'Forget the "or so". Let's say another year.'

'In that case when shall we announce the engagement?'

'Once you have bought me a ring.'

'By the time I have enough money to do that I should think we should be able to break the news to the breathless public at the same time that we shall put on *Pirates*.'

'What a good idea. The last-night party can be our engagement party. Frederick gets Mabel in the end.'

'Would you mind re-phrasing that?'

'Go and get that cup of tea, you naughty curate.'

Mrs Richards had placed the kettle on her gas stove in anticipation.

'I thought you two would be ready for a cup that says "Cheerio" as my husband used to say.'

As we sat on the floor in front of the fire with the two armchairs pulled up behind us and our cups of tea in our hands, I thought the time had come to refer to the subject of Charles and his infatuation.

'Speaking of engagements,' I said, 'you will be surprised to learn that Peter Pan has found a Wendy and has pledged his troth to her.'

'Stop speaking with forked tongue, Secombe, and explain what you mean about your colleague.'

'In other words, Charles has fallen, hook, line and sinker for Elspeth the sixteen-year-old blonde in the chorus and has informed me that he has become engaged to her.'

Eleanor stared at me in amazement.

'The idiot!' she exclaimed. 'That child is utterly promiscuous. I can't break my Hippocratic oath but I can tell you that she and her mother have been together in my surgery.'

'Thank you, my dear, that's all I want to know. I saw Elspeth in a close embrace with a school mate on a wall this afternoon. I should think even he will be convinced by your and my evidence that his romance is a non-starter.'

Next morning I went to call for Charles, ready to impart the information which I hoped would terminate the ill-starred love match. Myfanwy Howells opened the door.

'I'm afraid he's not very well. Emotionally upset, really.'

'What do you mean, Myfanwy?'

'Well, he came home after visiting with the Vicar, looking like death warmed up. After tea, he told me all about it. It seems he had fallen in love with that blonde girl in the chorus. Then when he was coming home with the Vicar, he saw her kissing and cuddling with a boy. He has gone off his food. No supper last night and feeling ill this morning.'

'Do you mind if I go upstairs to see him?'

'Not at all. You know his room.'

I knocked on his bedroom door.'

'Come in, Fred,' he shouted. The heartbroken curate was sitting up in bed. 'I thought you'd come up to see me. You were dead right about Elspeth. I saw her with my own eyes yesterday, kissing a kid her own age.'

'So did I, when I was coming back on the bus. Not only that but last night Eleanor told me to warn you against her. You've had a lucky escape. By the way, Myfanwy said you were feeling ill. You look all right to me.'

'When you knocked on the door just now, it was like the blinding light on the road to Damascus. That knock spelled out that another day of work had begun and that the world must go on. If you wait a minute downstairs, I'll be with you. Just put some talcum on my face to cover my stubble.'

When I reached the bottom of the stairs, Myfanwy was standing there.

'He has had a miraculous recovery,' I told her. 'Apparently my knock on your door was the blinding light on the road to Damascus.'

True to his word, in a minute or so he was coming downstairs, with more talcum on his cassock than on his face.

'You wouldn't believe it, would you?' said Myfanwy.

'You can believe anything about Charles. He's one big bundle of surprises,' I replied.

As we walked up the hill to the church my colleague produced another surprise out of his bundle.

'I think I'll get a dog for a companion. You can trust a dog.'

He never did get a dog.

13

'I'm calling a Parochial Church Council meeting for next week,' announced the Vicar at our Monday morning get together.

'We have only four more streets to survey. These will be done in the next few days. So I shall be able to let the Council know the results and enlist their support in a strategy of mission. Up to the present the percentage of population in Pontywen which is Anglican is forty-two-point-seven per cent. There are fifty-nine children unbaptised. We must remedy that situation for a start.'

'Are you envisaging a mass baptism, Vicar?' I asked.

'Something like that. It will make a big impact in Pontywen. The next news I have to report is that I have ordered a set of vestments for the parish church and for St Padarn's to be ready for Easter Day. I have decided to leave Llanhyfryd as it is for the time being.'

A look of relief crossed my fellow curate's face. He had been as terrified of wearing vestments as he had been of learning to drive the Vicar's car.

'Have you worn vestments before, Fred?' enquired the Vicar.

'Yes, on one occasion.' What I did not tell him was that the occasion was a complete fiasco.

The Vicar of my first parish had a habit of dispatching me to help out neighbouring incumbents. There was one Sunday when I was sent to preach for a Vicar who was more suited to a Gospel Hall than the Anglican Church. I received a public reprimand for referring to 'the altar' instead of to 'the holy table'. When I helped him with the administration of Holy Communion, the congregation said 'thank you' as I handed them the chalice, as if we were involved in some kind of picnic instead of the most sacred of all services.

Then at the other extreme was a church which was more ritualistic than a Roman Catholic church. The Vicar was absent on a pilgrimage to a shrine. When I arrived in the vestry, a server was engaged in preparing the incense ready for the service. The pungent smell of this aid to worship assaulted my nostrils. An elderly man in a cassock introduced himself to me as the MC. The only previous MCs I had met presided at ballroom dances I had attended.

'I'm afraid father's vestments are going to be a bit big for you,' he said when he saw me. 'He's well over six foot.'

'In that case,' I replied, 'at my height of five-foot-seven I am going to disappear inside his regalia.'

'Excuse me, Father. This is not a masonic ceremony you're dressing for. It is the holy sacrifice of the Mass.'

The little man was most indignant. His eyes flashed and his nostrils flared.

'My apologies for the "regalia" remark but you see, in my church, we are just dressed in cassock and surplice and stole. I have never worn vestments before.'

He stared at me in astonishment.

'Never worn vestments?'

'Never. Neither have I used incense. In fact the stuff gets on my chest.'

'It should clear your chest, Father – not get on it.'

'Whether it does or not, I don't care but what I do care about is making a fool of myself. If I start swinging that incense container, I shall be hitting the altar with it and perhaps yourself as well. So please count me out for that function. I shall put on the vestments but I am *not*, definitely *not*, using incense.'

He was speechless for a moment.

'Gareth,' he said to the server, 'you'd better stop preparing the incense. It's going to be a Low Mass.'

The MC opened a drawer in a chest of drawers, to reveal a set of vestments neatly arranged, amice, alb, girdle, stole and chasuble. I took off my jacket and put on my cassock.

'Now what do I do?' I asked the MC.

'First you put the amice over your head and tie the strings around you. I'll help you.'

The amice was a large square of white linen with strings attached to it. My head and most of my face was engulfed in this sheet while the master of ceremonies tied the strings around my middle.

'Next the alb, Father.'

I put on the long white linen robe. Gareth, the server, giggled and was rebuked by a hard look from the MC. There was an overflow of about three feet of linen on the floor while my hands were hidden away some two feet at least from the edge of the sleeves. What with the hood over my head, I looked like a member of the Ku-Klux-Klan who had bought the wrong size outfit.

'Let's see what we can do for you, Father. We'll get the girdle on you next.'

The long white rope was tied around my waist, with the tasselled ends dangling down to the floor. The little man proceeded to shorten the length by looping the ends through the circle around my waist. Next he pulled up the alb and tucked the three feet extra inside the girdle, giving an impression of pregnancy as the linen bulged out. Then he proceeded to fold back the sleeves to allow my hands to appear.

'Now the stole, Father.'

He put the stole around my neck and crossed it through the girdle.

'Now, last of all, Father, the chasuble.'

He took the large sleeveless green silk vestment, embroidered on the back with a long gold cross, in the form of a Y and slipped it over my head.

Once again my hands disappeared and the bottom of the vestment was perilously near my feet. It was a warm summer morning. What with the amice over my head and the excess of ceremonial clothing over my body, I felt stifled.

'This is mission impossible,' I said. 'How can I conduct a service, hidden away under all this.'

'Patience, Father,' chided the MC.

'Let's get the amice around your neck instead of your head.' So saying he pulled the linen square from my head and tucked it in around my neck like the sweat rags the tinplate workers used to wear going to their shift at the furnaces when I was a child in Swansea.

'At least I can see and breathe now but any movement is going to be well nigh impossible.'

'I'm sure you'll cope, Father.'

Cope I did not. Emerging from the vestry at the end of a long procession I got no further than a yard up the aisle, caught my foot in the alb which was slipping down already and fell forward on top of the MC. The two of us landed on the floor in an undignified heap. Eventually when I got to my feet, I said to

him, 'I'm going back into that vestry and I shall put on my surplice and stole. Otherwise there will be no service.' I was never asked to go there again.

'As you know,' said the Vicar, 'vestments are easy to put on.'

'That is, as long as they are the right size,' I added.

'Of course they will be the right size,' he snapped. 'I shall be informing the Council that we shall be wearing them on Easter Day.'

'I hope you will not meet with any great opposition,' I ventured to remark.

'Now look here, Fred, I want support from you and you, too, Wentworth-Baxter.'

Charles sat up as if suffering an electric shock. His mind had been elsewhere, possibly still behind the cemetery wall.

'If you don't mind me saying so, Vicar, you will have support from myself and Charles. It is not us you need worry about. Your headache will be supplied by people like Ezekiel Evans and Bertie Owen.'

'My apologies, Fred. I accept that I shall have your support for the introduction of vestments. Any change is bound to be regarded with suspicion. That's why I need your backing. As for Ezekiel Evans and especially Bertie Owen, I can easily deal with those idiots.'

It was with these words ringing in my ears that I walked down the Vicarage drive with my colleague.

'I think Father will soon find that Ezekiel and Bertie will not be the walkover he expects. Next week's meeting is going to be very interesting.'

When I told Mrs Richards about the vestments and what the Vicar had said about the lay reader and Bertie Owen, she forecast that he would have an unpleasant surprise.

'That Zekiel Evans is a connivling sort of man. He doesn't like it that his nose hasn't got a joint now that this new Vicar is here. He'll be round everybody behind the Vicar's back, stabbing him all the time, you wait and see.'

At two-thirty the clerical survey commenced in Ladysmith Terrace. Our folders with the vital statistical forms inside were becoming a familiar sight in the streets of Pontywen. Most of the population were mildly amused by the exercise. It was regarded as the new Vicar's eccentricity, something to be tolerated rather than admired.

I was detailed to do the odd numbers while Father Whittaker and Charles coped with the other side of the street. Number one had the blinds drawn. I knocked at the door and a lady in an ill-fitting black dress appeared. The smell from inside the house was horrendous.

'I'm glad you've come, Vicar,' she said. 'The undertaker sent you, was it?'

'As a matter of fact, it wasn't, but I'll come in all the same.'

When she closed the front door, the odour became positively

139

repulsive. She showed me into the sparsely furnished front room and invited me to sit in a grubby armchair.

'You've had a bereavement, Mrs – er ?'

'Watkins. My 'usband. 'E've 'ad cancer, getting worse and worse. Died this morning.'

'Well, I was on your doorstep because we are doing a survey of all the streets in Pontywen. I take it that you are Church of England.'

'Yes. Not that we go to church, mind.'

'How long has your husband been ill?'

'Oh, for about a year now but 'e's got terrible over the past few months. Dreadful. Would you like to come and see 'im, Vicar?'

'By the way, I'm not the Vicar. He's on the other side of the street. I'm the curate.'

'You'll do anyway. Would you like to follow me upstairs?'

It was obvious that she would not take no for an answer.

As we approached the bedroom, the stench became unbearable. She led me to the bed on which her late spouse reposed with a sheet over his face. When she removed it I was stricken with nausea, most of his face had been eaten away with cancer.

'You can see 'ow 'e's suffered,' she said, looking down at him.

'I can indeed.' I averted my eyes and moved towards the door. 'Would you like the Vicar to come and see you?'

'No, it's all right. One Vicar's as good as another. Will you do the funeral?'

'If you want me to.' By now I was outside the bedroom door, feeling violently sick.

'Yes, please,' she answered.

I went downstairs towards the front door, longing for the fresh air outside, even if it was the polluted variety supplied by Pontywen.

'I'll come and see you tomorrow, Mrs Watkins. In the meantime I'd better get on with the survey of the street.'

I opened the door and took a deep gulp of air.

'Thank you,' she said. 'I'll see you tomorrow.'

I closed the door, and stood outside, retching violently. The Vicar had just finished interviewing number four. He looked across at me and walked quickly towards me.

'What on earth is the matter, Fred? You look ghastly.'

I told him what had happened.

'I think you had better get back to your digs. You look as if you need a brandy. See you in the morning.'

So saying he knocked at number three and I made my way back to Mount Pleasant View.

Mrs Richards was surprised to see me.

'Mr Secombe you look terrible, whiter than a sheet.'

I repeated my story.

'The Vicar said I looked as if I needed a brandy.'

My landlady disappeared and came back with a small bottle of brandy.

'Mr Richards kept this in the house in case of accidents. Being a station master he had to be ready for every contingent. I've never opened it since he's gone. I'll get you a glass now.'

She came back with a tumbler and half filled it. 'There you are. You'll be completely renovated once you've drunk that.'

I sat in my armchair by the fire and began to sip the brandy. First my whole body felt warmed. Then my head began to feel so light that it could float away from my body, if it did not happen to be attached. The next stage was the magic roundabout which took control of my head. As it spun round I lost consciousness and fell into a deep sleep.

Several hours later I awoke to find my landlady standing over me.

'You've been in the land with Nod,' she said. 'But I tell you what, you do look a lot better.'

I did not like to tell her that far from being renovated I felt more suited to the scrap heap. The inside of my mouth was dry and tasted like the inside of a bird cage. My head was being attacked by little goblins with sledgehammers.

'What's the time, please?' I asked. 'Eleanor said she might be calling round.'

'It's half-past six. You'd better do your absolutions and smarten yourself up before she comes.'

Mrs Richards made my personal hygiene sound like a stint in the confessional box.

I crawled upstairs and put my head under the cold water tap. It was a drastic remedy but it worked. I felt refreshed and ready to meet my beloved who arrived promptly at seven o'clock.

'What has afflicted you, Frederick?' she asked.

141

'You should have seen me at three o'clock,' I said. I recounted my cancer victim experience for the third time.

'As I have said before, you'll never make a doctor. But it must have been a shock to see that sight when you are not prepared for it. The widow had been looking at her husband's face for months not realising how dreadful it would appear to an outsider. Still, cheer up, I bring you tidings of great joy.'

'I know you're an angel, love, but would you mind defining the tidings?'

'My employer, Dr Elias Llewellyn Hughes, whom you admire so much, has given me a rise of two hundred and fifty pounds a year.'

'That rise is ten pounds more than my annual pay.'

'If you will choose the wrong profession, my love.'

'Excuse me. I have chosen the right profession but the wrong pay. The little woman who kept the post office in Swansea where my mother collected my father's war pension used to tell her that I should "go in for being a doctor rather than a Vicar". My mother always replied that caring for souls was more important than caring for bodies. Miss Jacobs, who was deputy organist at the parish church, would then say that bodies paid more than souls. She was right, obviously.'

'Do you think we could discuss this deep philosophical theme over dinner? I have come to invite you to a meal to celebrate my new-found wealth.'

'Despite my delicate state of health, I shall be delighted to accept on condition that you will give me time to dash upstairs and put on my best suit with collar and tie to match.'

'I should dab a little rouge on your cheeks while you're up there.'

She drove down the valley to the one four-star hotel in the vicinity. The dining room was almost full. There was one table for two left. We were in a corner where we could observe our fellow diners one of whom, eating alone, was someone I recognised. He was Daniel Fitzgerald, a solicitor who was the Diocesan registrar. A plump red-faced man wearing horn-rimmed spectacles, he was attacking his main course with obvious relish.

'He's eating enough food for two,' I said discreetly indicating his whereabouts. 'That's old Fitzgerald. He's a pompous individual, Diocesan registrar.'

The words were hardly out of my mouth before he was convulsed with a choking fit. His face went purple and he was fighting for breath.

Eleanor was away from her chair like a greyhound out of the traps. She went to him and put her fingers down his throat pulling out a piece of stringy meat which had threatened his life. For the second time that day my stomach heaved violently. She put the offending gristle on his side plate and made a quick exit to the ladies cloakroom.

When she returned, having washed her hands and powdered her nose, the old man came to our table.

'Young lady, I wish to thank you for your prompt action. You have probably saved my life.'

'Mr Fitzgerald, I can vouch for that, as a doctor. A matter of seconds and you could have choked to death.'

'All the more reason to be grateful. By the way how did you know my name? And if I may be so bold, may I know yours?'

'I know your name because my friend here is a curate at Pontywen and apparently you are a Diocesan official. My name is Eleanor Davies and I work with Dr Hughes in Pontywen.'

'Mr Secombe, I don't think we have met.' I stood up and he shook my hand. 'What a fortunate young man you are to have such a charming and resourceful young lady as your friend. May I thank you once more, Dr Davies, for being an angel of mercy?'

As he went back to his table I said to Eleanor, 'It's not everybody who is called an angel twice in the same day.'

'It's not everybody who has an escort who works for the same firm as the angels.'

'Speaking of that firm and of the low wage it pays its workers, how on earth am I going to keep you in the style to which you are accustomed?'

'My dear Fred, marriage is a union of two equal partners. You are living in the twentieth century not the middle ages. I am not a shrinking violet to be fed and watered by her lord and master. Believe me, I have no intention of giving up my profession when I marry you. What I earn will go into the common purse.'

'In that case I must stay with Father Whittaker for three or four years at least. By then I should be in line for a living somewhere, not too far from Pontywen if you want to stay with Dr Hughes.'

'I know you don't like the old man because of his opposition to our relationship. He has dropped that now. He's too dependent on me to do anything else. What is more, it will not be long before he will be asking me to come into partnership with him. So I'm afraid, my love, you will have to stick with Father for quite a while.'

'Well at least he is not as unbearable as he threatened to be, mainly because of you. He is such a social climber. To think that his curate is courting a doctor is a boost for his ego. All will be well as long as he controls his itch to go the whole hog and introduce incense, sanctuary bells and High Mass, et cetera. I'm afraid I should have to move if he gets carried away.'

'I think you'll find there will be such opposition to vestments that he'll think twice about incense. Don't forget I was born and bred in Pontywen and I know the people. They don't like being pushed around. I like them and I'm only too pleased to know that before long I shall be living among them.'

She took my hand and squeezed it.

'If we are going to get married next year it means we shall have to begin to think of where we are going to live. You know what the housing shortage is like.'

With the men returning from the forces and with no house building during the war years, accommodation was in extremely short supply. Any empty house was in danger of being occupied by squatters.

'Between us,' she said, 'what with you and your contacts with parishioners and me and my patients, we should be able to find something, be it ever so humble.'

Mr Fitzgerald arose from his table at that moment and waved a goodbye to us before he left.

'There you are,' said Eleanor. 'You called him a pompous individual but he may be the means of you becoming a Vicar earlier than you think. Cast your bread upon the water.'

'It's a waterfall, according to Mrs Richards.'

'Water or waterfall, you never know what a kindness may bring in return.'

'I never thought you were so calculating.'

'With a husband-to-be like you, my dear, calculating will be a necessity on my part.'

144

14

The atmosphere in the parish church hall was as convivial as a get-together between miners' leaders and colliery managers. It was obvious that the first Parochial Church Council meeting under the chairmanship of the new Vicar was going to be a stormy one.

Seated at the table, apparently examining the minutes book with great interest, was the Vicar, clad in his cassock and cape. Roving around the various members of the Council was Ezekiel Evans indulging in conspiratorial whispers. Since the arrival of Father Whittaker the lay reader was virtually unemployed, apart from reading a lesson occasionally. His heart was bitter within him. Nothing would give him greater pleasure than to see the new incumbent in deep trouble at this meeting.

In the corner of the hall by the door was someone else who shared the same feelings. Bertie Owen was in loud and earnest conversation with three members of St Padarn's. One sentence which reached the ears of Charles and myself at our seats in the front was ominous. 'I'm not standing for any changes.'

A few minutes later the Vicar rapped on the table with a coin. 'Will you all take your seats, please?' Bertie and the others who were standing made their way, grimfaced, to the vacant chairs. The secretary of the Council, Sam Thomas, a clerk in the colliery office, joined the Vicar who asked everybody to stand for prayers.

'Oolmighty Gad,' was addressed for five minutes giving rise to a certain amount of shuffling from Bertie's direction and a few sighs from behind me. The minutes of the last meeting were read by the secretary at express speed. Since he suffered from a Churchillian impediment in his speech his reading was more noteworthy for its showers of spray rather than its intelligibility.

'Will someone propose we accept the minutes as a true record?' asked the Vicar.

'Did you read my name out as being present?' enquired Bertie Owen of the secretary.

'On a point of order,' said the Vicar, 'would you mind addressing the secretary through the Chair?'

'I was only asking him if he read my name out. He goes so fast you can't understand what he was saying. As for points of order, I know all about them. I'm not a shop steward for nothing. Points of order, Mr Chairman, are about important things not just about whether you were at a meeting.'

'Points of order, Mr Owen, are about procedural matters. At a meeting the procedure is that you always address everybody through the Chair and not directly – even if it is simply to enquire if your name had been omitted from those present at the last meeting.'

'Now look here, Vicar, don't you tell me about how to run meetings. I've been to more meetings than you've had hot dinners.'

At this point Sam Thomas leaned across to the Vicar and whispered something.

'Mr Owen, your name *was* read out as being present at the last meeting. Now let us proceed. I have a number of important subjects to discuss. First the parish survey.'

'Excuse me, Mr Chairman, on a point of order.' It was Bertie again. 'We haven't passed a motion accepting the minutes of the last meeting yet.'

The Vicar's face was scarlet.

'Will someone please propose we accept the minutes as a true record of the last meeting?'

There was a long and embarrassing pause. Then Vaughan-Jenkins, the people's Warden, put up his hand.

'Proposed by Mr Jenkins.'

'Who will second it?'

This time Harold Jones, the Vicar's Warden, indicated his willingness to second the motion.

'All those in favour.' All hands went up.

'Now then shall we get down to business? We have completed the parish survey.'

146

'Excuse me, Mr Chairman, on a point of order,' Bertie was on his feet again.

Father Whittaker's patience was approaching the exhaustion stage.

'What now, Mr Owen?'

'You haven't put it to the meeting if there were any matters arising from the minutes.'

'Are there any matters arising from the minutes? If not I should like to proceed with the meeting?'

Ezekiel Evans was on his feet.

'Mr Chairman, h'as Mr h'Owen 'as said, h'inasmuch h'as the secretary was reading the minutes so quickly, h'it was difficult to h'understand what 'e was saying. 'Owever h'I think h'I gathered that there was talk of h'a memorial to h'our late beloved Vicar. H'inasmuch as h'I 'ave 'eard nothing more h'about it, can you tell us h'if anything 'as been done with reference to this – er memorial?'

The Vicar contemplated the green baize cloth on the table in front of him. He seemed to be taking deep breaths. When his breathing exercises were over, he raised his head and glared at Ezekiel Evans through his horn-rimmed spectacles.

'Nothing has been done as yet. I have been giving a great deal of thought to it and I shall discuss the matter with the Council at the next meeting. It will have to be a permanent memorial of some kind but in the meanwhile there is a less permanent memorial already donated which I shall mention later in this meeting. Now is there any other matter arising from the minutes?'

It was more of a challenge than a question. The malcontents decided to bide their time.

'I take it that there are no more questions about the last meeting. As I was saying earlier, there are a number of vitally important matters of parochial strategy I want to raise this evening. The parish survey has been completed. I am grateful to Father Secombe and Father Wentworth-Baxter for their help in this task.'

Sixteen pairs of eyebrows were raised at the elevation to fatherhood of Charles and myself.

'The result of the survey shows that forty-four-point-seven per cent of the population are Anglican, forty-two-point-five-six are non conformist, eight-point-nine-seven per cent are Roman Catholic and the other three-point-seven-four per cent are agnostic.'

'So what,' muttered Bertie.

'Did you say something, Mr Owen?' The tone was that of the Church militant.

'Mr Chairman,' undaunted, Bertie rose to his feet, 'I don't know what all these points have got to do with us. It seems to me you've been wasting your time. Most of us have been born and bred in Pontywen and we know who's who, without having to go round asking.'

'Hear, hear!' chorused a number of voices.

'We have not been wasting our time, Mr Owen. Did you know that there are fifty-seven children needing baptism in this parish? Did you know that at least seventy-five per cent of those who claimed to be Anglican don't come to church?'

'I could have told you that without going round with paper and pencil. So what are you going to do about it?'

The Vicar could not believe his luck.

'That, Mr Owen, is the whole point of this meeting. So would you mind sitting down and listening to what I have to say?'

Bertie's brain could stand the strain of competition with that of the Vicar no longer. He subsided into his chair.

'First of all, baptisms. The clergy will visit all those houses where there are unbaptised children. We hope to arrange a big service when all or most of these infants will be baptised. This should make a big impact on Pontywen.'

'Secondly, I propose to have a series of social gatherings, with a cup of tea and a biscuit, to which we shall invite all the families in a set number of streets who claim to be Anglican but never come. At these gatherings we shall have those who come to church from that list of streets to act as hosts and hostesses.'

The Vicar leaned back in his chair, looking pleased with himself and waiting to have the seal of approval for these beginnings of a parochial strategy. There was a pregnant silence in which a batch of objections struggled for birth.

Inevitably it was Bertie's which saw the light of day first.

'Mr Chairman, I think you're in for a big surprise with these baptisms. If they haven't had them done by now, what makes

148

you think they'll bring the kids along simply because you've arranged a service.'

'That's right, Mr Chairman,' said Jim Evans, past Church-warden. 'You can take an 'orse to the water but you can't make 'im drink.'

'The same h'applies to your bunfight, Mr Chairman.' Ezekiel joined in the disapproval with relish. 'H'if you think a cup of tea and a biscuit will bring them to the church 'all, h'I'm afraid you're going to 'ave an h'unpleasant surprise, h'as Mr h'Owen said about the baptisms, h'inasmuch h'as 'uman nature h'is what it h'is.'

I felt sorry for the Chairman. His parochial strategy was in shreds already.

Three members of the Council rose to their feet and voiced their opposition to the new ideas.

Father Whittaker looked a beaten man and as yet he had not broached the subject of vestments.

'I can see that you feel that these two suggestions I have made are doomed to failure. However, we can but try and I hope that you will give us your co-operation despite your misgivings.' The militancy had gone from his tone of voice to be replaced by a note of resignation.

'Now then, I come to something I mentioned briefly earlier in the meeting. A person who wishes to be anonymous has given me a generous donation to buy something in memory of the late Canon Llewellyn. With it I have bought a set of vestments for the parish church and for St Padarn's.'

I nudged Charles, as we waited for the reaction. This time it was immediate. A number of members rose to their feet.

'One at a time, please. Mr Vaughan-Jenkins you were the first to stand.' The Vicar's face was ashen. His colour was changing so often that it would have made a chameleon envious.

'Two things, Mr Chairman. The least you could have done was to let the two Wardens of the parish church know that you had been given a donation to buy something in memory of the late Vicar. That's the first thing. The second is that as Canon Llewellyn never wore vestments, I don't think he would have wanted money wasted on them anyway.'

'I'm next, Mr Chairman.' Bertie was not waiting to be called. 'We don't want this dressing up in St Padarn's. We've never had

149

it before and I don't see why we should start now. The next thing is we'll be like Our Lady of Lourdes down the road. Once you start there'll be no end to it. I tell you what, Mr Chairman, there'll be a strike in our church if you push this thing down our throats.'

Ezekiel Evans added his contribution. 'Mr Chairman, h'in-asmuch h'as I 'ave been lay reader in Pontywen for the past twelve years h'I think h'I know the feeling of the people towards such a big h'alteration in the worship. You'll 'ave an h'empty church, believe me.'

The onslaught continued from several others who felt constrained to speak. There was not one voice raised in favour of the wearing of vestments. In the face of this total opposition, the Vicar was forced to capitulate.

'I have no wish to foist anything on an unwilling congregation,' he said wearily. 'For the time being the vestments will remain in mothballs. Perhaps in the fullness of time, attitudes will change. Will you all stand and we shall finish the meeting with the blessing.'

The Council members trooped out in jubilant mood with Bertie Owen swelling with pride, almost expecting to be carried out shoulder-high like a Welsh Captain after a famous victory at Cardiff Arms Park.

Ezekiel Evans came up to the Vicar as he sat at the table with his shoulders drooped.

'H'I 'ope you didn't mind, Vicar, but h'I felt h'I 'ad to h'express public h'opinion.'

'Of course, Mr Evans.'

At least Father Whittaker was not vindictive in defeat.

'He should have been called Judas Evans,' whispered Charles to me.

'I agree,' I replied, 'and this meeting should be known as Whittaker's Waterloo.'

As the lay reader left, the Vicar rose from the table and came across to us.

'I had set my heart on coming to Pontywen,' he said, 'because it was the one parish in the Valley where I thought I could exercise my priestly ministry to the full. Evidently I made a mistake. Canon Llewellyn had taken them so far in the Catholic tradition. It appears he knew when to stop. I suppose I could

150

carry on as I intended and empty the church. There are priests who have done that. They end up lonely and embittered men. I don't intend to do that, but, I tell you what, we are going to go ahead with the baptisms and we shall have them on the afternoon of Easter Day.'

Next morning after our daily service we met in the Vicarage for an inquest on the previous evening's events. By now the Vicar had recovered his equilibrium.

'We have three weeks to prepare for the mass baptisms on Easter Day. I propose we begin at once to visit the homes of the unbaptised children and by the end of the week we shall have some idea of how many will respond to our invitation.'

Charles and I were given twelve houses each to visit. As we left the Vicarage, Charles attempted his usual ploy.

'Why don't we do the houses together? You know what I'm like. If you were with me, I wouldn't get trapped.'

'Charles,' I said. 'You sound like a young rabbit talking to its father. I am not your father and it's time you stopped being a rabbit. You do your twelve and I shall do mine, as instructed by our superior.'

He went off in high dudgeon to his digs while I made my way to the first address on my list as a prelude to my lunch. Number seven Richmond Crescent seemed to indicate a house in the up-market end of Pontywen. It turned out to be a semi-detached council house with a wilderness of a garden and a wooden gate clinging perilously by one hinge to a concrete post.

According to my list there were two children to be baptised, Marilyn aged three months and Shirley aged two. As I approached the front door I could hear a baby wailing and a woman's voice screeching at Shirley for some misdemeanour.

I was in two minds about knocking on the door. After a pause for thought I decided to risk a knock. I rapped the knocker.

'Who the hell is that now?' screamed the mother, listed as Mrs Watkins.

She charged up the passage and flung open the door. The expression on her face indicated a mixture of surprise, embarrassment and displeasure in equal proportions. Mrs Watkins was a lady in her late thirties, clad in a none too clean dress which had split at the seams underneath her arms and whose hair had not been in contact with a brush that day.

151

'Kids!' she exploded. 'To think how much I wanted 'em. I wish I'd known what it's like. I'd never 'ave 'ad 'em.'

Shirley emerged from the front room, looking as dishevelled as her mother.

'Get back in there, our Shirley, and close the door.' The little girl disappeared in a flash.

'It's – er – about the children that I've called,' I said limply. 'We're having a baptism at the parish church on Easter Day at three p.m. and the Vicar was wondering if you would like to bring them along.'

'Look, love,' she spoke to me as if I were Shirley's age, 'you can see what this place is like. I can't afford to buy new clothes for my kids to go to your church nor to 'ave a party after. Tell the Vicar that, will you?'

She closed the door firmly and went back to scolding Shirley who had dared to leave the front room for the second time. My first assignment had been a pointless exercise.

'I'm beginning to feel a bit sorry for the Vicar,' said Mrs Richards when I told her what had happened. 'He's really going under the mill at the moment, isn't he? He's finding out what Pontywen is like. To try all these new mangled ideas is like a red flag to a bull here. He'll learn, I'm sure.'

By the end of the week he had learned the lesson which Jim Evans had forecast, 'You can take an 'orse to the water but you can't make 'im drink.' Of the fifty-seven who were to be brought to the water of baptism only eleven children had been booked for the ceremony. 'The big impact' heralded by the Vicar was to have as little impression as 'hitting a wall with a wet tram ticket', as Idris the Milk would put it.

On Sunday morning after service at St Padarn's, Bertie Owen was jubilant when I told him that the number of children to be baptised was eleven and not fifty-seven.

'I told him he was wasting his time,' he crowed. 'The sooner he goes from Pontywen the better.'

'Bertie,' I said, 'you're a fine Christian! You should be sad that so few people want to bring their children to be christened. Not only that, but if you think the Vicar is going to get out of Pontywen very soon, you're making a big mistake.'

'I thought you were on our side.' He looked at me as if I had been bought by thirty pieces of silver.

'If by that you mean that I don't want Pontywen to become an Anglo-Catholic centre in the Valleys, you are right. That's far different from wanting our parish to be a live one and being prepared to see changes to make that happen. I'm all for anything which is going to improve church life in Pontywen.'

'Hear! Hear!' said Idris from inside the surplice he was taking off. On reappearing, he launched into an attack on Bertie. 'We've had enough warfare to keep us going for donkey's years without starting another war in Pontywen. Now that you've had your little victory, Bertie, there's no need to rub the Vicar's nose in it.'

The Churchwarden looked like a little boy who had been sent into the corner by his schoolteacher.

Any further discussion of the subject was cut short by the sudden appearance in the vestry of Eleanor, her face flushed with excitement.

'Do you mind if I kidnap your curate?' she said to Bertie and Idris.

'I'm sure they wouldn't,' I replied, speaking on their behalf only too pleased to see an end to Bertie's discomfiture.

In no time at all we were in her car.

'Now before you drive off, perhaps you would explain your invasion of my vestry,' I demanded in mock indignation.

'Well, it's like this, your worship.' She touched her forelock where it would have been, had she possessed one. 'How would you like to marry me within the next six months?'

I stared at her, my mouth agape.

'I know it's not leap-year,' she went on, 'but something has turned up that I don't think we should turn down.'

'Are you being serious?' I managed to say.

'Of course I'm being serious, Frederick, and pray don't look so startled. I've just come from the hospital where Miss Bradshaw has passed away at last. Now it so happens that her landlord is a friend of my father's. I'm sure he would let it to us.'

'Miss Bradshaw's house!' I exploded. 'It's a slum. It needs fumigation. It – it's absolutely filthy.'

Miss Bradshaw was an eccentric who lived in a house full of old newspapers and cats. I had called in Eleanor when I discovered her lying unconscious amidst her squalor. For months

153

she had been hovering between life and death in the hospital.

'Look, my dear. You know what the housing situation is like. Men are coming back from the forces with nowhere to live. If we wait to find somewhere to live we may have to wait for years. There is nothing wrong with the house. When it has been cleaned and redecorated it will be ideal as a first home for us.'

'But, it's not just getting a house. It must have furniture. I have just a few pounds in my post office savings account and what is that among so many commitments?'

'Fred!' her tone was sharp. 'Do you love me?'

'Of course, you know that but –'

'No more buts! At the moment I am in a position to help furnish the house. One day we shall be in a Vicarage and your stipend will be much bigger than it is now. Then you can take over. So, please, please, let me do my share while I can.'

By now there were a few interested spectators from the choir standing outside the church gate, pretending to talk to each other.

'I think we had better move,' I suggested.

She turned the ignition key and put her foot down on the accelerator as if a chequered flag had been raised.

'Where are we going?' I enquired.

'To The Hawthorns, where we have an appointment with Mr Lloyd-Evans, owner of eleven, Bevans Row. I phoned him from the hospital.'

'Eleanor!' I gasped.

'Eleanor, what?'

'The poor old girl had only just breathed her last and you were on the phone straight away.'

'In this life, my love, if you want something, you won't get it by sitting down and waiting for it to happen. You have to be up and away. That's why we're going now.'

The Hawthorns was a mansion, greystoned and forbidding in appearance, perched on the hillside away from the mean streets of Pontywen. It was screened from the road by the tall fir trees which lined the winding drive and the rolling lawns.

By the time we reached the front door I had been given a brief biography of Mr Lloyd-Evans. He was a solicitor, a county councillor and a property owner. Born and bred in the same mining village as Eleanor's father, he was a self-made local tycoon. Now in his seventies he was a widower and was cared for by a housekeeper, 'a bit of a dragon', according to Eleanor.

She pulled hard on the handle of the antiquated doorbell which echoed its clang around the hall.

'This reminds me of one of those horror films. Any minute now a butler called Death will open the door,' I said.

She giggled.

'You'll see his female counterpart any second.'

Right on cue the door was opened slowly with the appropriate creaking.

A grey-haired, gaunt featured, unsmiling lady in black confronted us. The aroma of a Sunday roast drifted from the kitchen and destroyed the image of spookery.

'Mr Lloyd-Evans is waiting for you in the drawing room.' She spoke with a thick Valleys accent out of character with her appearance.

We were ushered into the drawing room where a white-haired little man with a bushy white moustache came to greet Eleanor with a kiss.

'Well, what are you up to now?' he asked with a smile on his face.

'First of all,' she replied, catching hold of my hand, 'this is my future husband.'

He grasped my hand firmly and looked into my eyes.

'You're a better man than I am, Gunga Din.' He released his grip. 'You realise that you have a little atom bomb in this child. It's a good thing you are a man of the cloth. Ordinary mortals could never control her.'

'Thank you, Uncle Frank,' she said and made a deep curtsey.

'Well, well! You wish to take over from where Miss Bradshaw left off. You realise what a heritage she has left you.'

'You mean, a small fortune in old newspapers and a potential holiday home for cats.'

'What I mean, my dear, is a load of filth and acres of dust.'

'As a reasonable man you will realise that you could not let that house to any tenant, however desperate, without having it cleaned and redecorated from top to bottom.'

He fixed his penetrating gaze on her eyes, being met by an equal intensity from her direction. There was a long pause.

'You win, you bully. You should know better than to batter

155

an old man into submission. There's one proviso. Don't expect anything to be done immediately.'

'As long as it's done within the next six months, I shan't say a word. I shall be only too grateful.'

She gave the old man a peck on the cheek.

'Let's celebrate the agreement with a sherry. Dry, medium or sweet?' He moved across to the drinks cabinet.

'Dry,' we chorused.

'Good to know you're in harmony. May it always be so.' As he poured out the drinks he said to me 'How long will it be before you get your own parish and your own Vicarage?'

'At least another three or four years. Probably longer.'

He handed the glasses of sherry to Eleanor and me and then poured out one for himself.

'Here's to your three or four years in eleven, Bevan's Row. May they be happy and healthy.'

We drank to that toast. Then he added, 'knowing your job they certainly will not be wealthy.'

'At least, Mr Lloyd-Evans, I can say that Eleanor is not marrying me for my money.'

'You will find, my boy, that money is not everything.'

'I remember having to write an essay,' I said, 'which was entitled, "The love of money may be the root of all evil but the want of it is the whole blooming tree". At the moment all I can see is a tree. Eleanor assures me that the tree isn't there.'

'If Eleanor says the tree isn't there,' he replied, 'then you can take her word for it. It isn't.'

On our way back to my digs we stopped for a kiss and a cuddle.

'Have you told your parents?' I asked as she was about to resume driving.

'That's a pleasant surprise they've got coming to them this afternoon. It wouldn't be a bad idea if you wrote and told your parents as well.'

'And I thought this Sunday was just going to be another Sunday,' I said.

15

Eleanor's invasion of the vestry on Passion Sunday was a watershed in my life in Pontywen. After that morning, events seemed to rush by me as if in a speeded up film. Both sets of parents acknowledged that in six months or so their children would be wed. Both mothers were concerned that so much had to happen in so short a time. Both fathers were content to let both mothers do the worrying.

In the meanwhile Easter came and went. The grand baptismal event fizzled out into a ceremony involving nine children. At the Easter vestry meeting Bertie Owen was elected once again as people's Warden of St Padarn's despite the fervent prayers of the Vicar. A further headache for Father Whittaker was the call for a revival of the Whitsun Treat after the lapse of the war years. Inevitably this meant that Bertie Owen offered himself as organiser. Since no one else wanted the job, he was elected but with unanimous misgivings on the part of those who elected him.

The traditional Whitsun treat used to take place on Whit Monday after a big procession of Sunday School children to the parish church on Sunday. This was the time when parents bought new clothes for their children. For some it was their only outing in the year, their one journey in a train. The more affluent Sunday Schools took their pupils to Barry Island for a day at the funfairs and the seaside. Pontywen parish transported their contingent to a wayside halt further up the valley in the countryside where they hired a field for the day.

When I announced in Sunday School at St Padarn's that there was to be a Whitsun treat, the excitement was intense.

'Are we going to 'ave races?' enquired Tommy Harris.

'I expect so,' I said. 'Is that right, Mr Owen?' Bertie was standing alongside me, looking very important.

'Of course we're having races. We always have races.'

'Will there be prizes?' persisted Tommy, who fancied himself to win all his races.

'Of course,' replied Bertie. 'Threepence first prize, twopence for second and a penny for third.'

'I can beat you,' Percy, son of Idris the Milk, challenged Tommy. 'I bet you.'

'That's enough of that,' I shouted above the hubbub that ensued. 'Mr Owen has got something else to say to you.'

'Now then, boys and girls, will you ask your parents if they can spare a few sweet coupons? We'd like to give you all a packet of sweets when you come into the field on Whit Monday. You can bring them over the next few Sundays,' announced Bertie.

For the rest of the afternoon, the excitement was so intense it was difficult to keep discipline. While I was marking the register the private war between Tommy and Percy continued and it was not confined to races.

'I'm going to sit next to Betty Evans. You wait till we come to the tunnels,' Tommy boasted to Percy.

Betty Evans was a pretty little girl and obviously a prize possession.

'Now, watch it, Tommy or you'll be getting a bunch of fives. She's my girl.' Percy raised his fist. Since he had been given a part in *The Pirates of Penzance* his self confidence had increased considerably.

'Will you two be quiet? Otherwise I shall put you to sit with the girls this afternoon since that seems to matter so much to you.'

My threat proved to be most effective. The two boys contented themselves with glaring at each other from time to time and with trying to outshout each other in singing the last hymn:

> Lamb of God, I look to thee,
> Thou shalt my example be.

'Well, Bertie,' I said, after the children had left. 'What other arrangements are involved?'

'I've been down to the station and seen Mr Wilkinson the

Station master. We've got a special train booked with six coaches and I've seen Mr Pugh, the farmer, about the field. As long as we leave the field as we found it, he'll be quite happy.'

'What about the catering? There'll be a fair amount of mouths to fill, let alone the stomachs of Tommy Harris, et cetera.'

'As far as making tea is concerned, we've got the boiler at the parish church. Mr Hopkins always sees to that. We'll take it on the back of Minty the Coal's lorry together with the crockery and the food.'

Reuben Hopkins was superintendent of the Sunday School at the parish church. He was a tall man with a black moustache big enough to fit on a broom handle. Idris the Milk had informed me that he was the man whose stomach used to rumble when he stood in the queue to receive Holy Communion at the early service. Apparently he used to turn around and look at the person behind him as if he or she were responsible for the breach of the peace. A further tit-bit of gossip from Idris was to the effect that Reuben was renowned for telling the dirtiest stories in the steelworks, where he worked at the furnaces.

The 'boiler' was a contraption I had noted when I first came to Pontywen. Situated at the back of the parish church it looked like Stevenson's Rocket, the original model. Rusty and coated with a thick layer of Pontywen grime it had a tall thin funnel with a boiler attached. When I saw it I had asked if it were a monument to the early days of the railway in the Valleys.

Over the next few Sundays, attendance at Sunday School increased dramatically. Lost sheep returned to the fold bringing strays from Tabernacle Baptist and Bethel Congregational with them, neither Chapel having a Sunday School treat that year.

Whit Sunday morning was sunny and warm. According to Mrs Richards this was divinely ordained. 'Every time we have a lovely day for the procession and for the Whitsun treat. As the old Canon used to say the sun always laughed at the righteous. It will be beautiful again tomorrow, you see. We must be a very fanatical lot in Pontywen.'

The Vicar had arranged to have the Salvation Army band from Cwmtydfil to lead the procession to the parish church. All the children and teachers were to meet at St Padarn's by 2.30 p.m. and then walk the half mile to St Mary's, walking in pairs, behind the band.

By 2.20 p.m. chaos reigned supreme as teachers sought out their classes from the two hundred or so children milling around excitedly, the girls preening themselves in their new summer dresses and the boys in their new suits, indulging in mock fights to impress the girls. Evidently there had been an avalanche of clothing coupons deposited in the shops of Pontywen, Newport and Cardiff over the past week.

At 2.25 p.m. the parish choir in cassock and surplice arrived, led by Will Thomas, a burly sixteen-year-old, carrying the processional cross, the Vicar and Charles Wentworth-Baxter, in their robes, bringing up the rear. They joined the St Padarn's choir who were under the control of Mr Collier the organist and choirmaster, or, to be more exact, were not under the control of Mr Collier.

It became apparent immediately that the two sets of choirboys regarded each other with as much love as the Welsh and English supporters at the Arms Park.

'Where is the Salvation Army band?' demanded the Vicar.

'I'm afraid they've not turned up yet,' I replied.

'They were supposed to be here at a quarter-past two,' he said petulantly.

'Where are the songs of spring? Where are they?' I murmured.

'What's that?' the Vicar said.

'I wonder where they are,' I replied.

'Wentworth-Baxter, get back to the parish church as quickly as you can and tell the organist to be prepared to play the hymns instead of the band. Then get back here.'

Charles looked as happy as an unfit athlete who found that he had to run an extra mile because of a miscalculation.

At a quarter-to-three the procession was in a state of mayhem with the boys of the parish church in violent contention with the boys of St Padarn's, urged on by the girls of both camps. Bertie Owen and Reuben Hopkins were involved in a heated altercation as to which set of boys was responsible for the trouble. The Vicar was just in time to prevent Will Thomas, the crossbearer, from using the sacred symbol as a weapon of war.

'Quiet!' shouted Father Whittaker. He was wasting his breath. Confusion still reigned supreme.

'Fred. Can you do something to end this disgraceful behaviour?' He had reached the end of his tether.

I was about to wade into the fray when the bus supplied by Evans Luxury Transport, Cwmtydfil groaned into sight. It was like the relief of Mafeking.

'Sorry about the 'itch in the arrangements, Vicar,' said the bandmaster as he stepped out of the coach. 'A breakdown after we'd gone a few miles. They 'ad to send out another bus.'

It took another ten minutes for the band to organise themselves. Eventually the procession moved off half an hour late to the appropriate strains of 'Onward Christian Soldiers, marching as to war, with the Cross of Jesus going on before.'

'Isn't it about time that Wentworth-Baxter was back here?' The Vicar and I were marching behind the two choirs. The sun had come out and it was quite a warm afternoon. Father Whittaker looked uncomfortable in the large black cloak which enveloped his robes.

'I expect he'll join us any time now,' I replied. 'It looks as if we are going to have a lovely day for tomorrow's treat.' I should not have said that. It was like rubbing salt into a wound.

He glared at me.

'I don't care if it snows tomorrow and we have to cancel it. I've had enough already,' he growled.

There was still no sign of Charles by the time that we reached the parish church.

'I expect he's inside,' I said to the Vicar.

He was not inside.

Half-way through the service Charles tottered up the aisle in a state of semi-collapse, to the great amusement of Idris and company but not the Vicar.

'Where have you been?' he demanded.

'I must have missed you,' gasped my colleague who then collapsed into his seat in the middle of 'The Church's one foundation'.

'And you still have the Sunday School treat tomorrow,' I said to him, out of the side of my mouth.

He gave me a look which was decidedly unChristian.

The Vicar gave the choirboys and the Sunday School children a lecture about their bad behaviour and threatened to cancel all future outings if there was a repeat performance at the treat. The next morning after the service he gave Charles a lecture on the need for common sense in a priest's ministry and forecast a catalogue of misfortunes in the day ahead since Bertie Owen was in charge.

'The man has all the arrogance of ignorance,' he said, 'and all the trouble it brings with it. The only thing we can do today is to try to minimise its effects.'

The children were due to meet at their Sunday Schools at 11.30 a.m., where they would be given their tickets and proceed in a crocodile to Pontywen Station where the special train was due to leave at 12.10 p.m. Parents who were coming to the outing would get their tickets at the station.

There was no sign of Bertie Owen at 11.30 a.m. by which time all the children and their teachers were assembled. At 11.35 a.m. Bertie arrived, looking flustered, and carrying a suitcase.

'I've just seen off Minty's lorry, Reuben Hopkins was late coming to see to the loading of the boiler. We've got all the trestle tables on the lorry and all the food for the women to cut up. So they should be in the field by the time we arrive.'

'That's OK, Bertie,' I said. 'We'd better get cracking with giving out the tickets. Otherwise it's going to be a bit of a rush.'

He opened the suitcase which was full of bags of sweets and rummaged through the contents. Gradually the colour drained from his face.

'The tickets must be on top of our piano. I gave the parish church their lot yesterday and I put ours on one side. Then I got busy packing the sweets and I must have forgotten to put in the tickets. I'll go and get them now and come back.'

'There's no time for that,' I snapped. 'Give me the case. Get back home as fast as you can and go direct to the station. We'll take the children to the station and they can wait outside the station gates.'

'Right you are, Mr Secombe. Good thinking. I'll be at the station by the time you arrive with the children.'

'Promises, promises,' said Idris the Milk. 'What with 'im and Charles they couldn't organise a what-you-call in a brewery, if you know what I mean.'

'I know what you mean, Idris, but let's get moving.'

'We arrived at the station at 12 o'clock to be greeted by the Vicar who demanded to know where we had been.

'Your forecast this morning is coming true, Vicar. Bertie has forgotten to bring the tickets. He'll be here any time now.'

'I knew it. I knew it,' he spluttered. 'This isn't a bus we're travelling on. You can't hold back a train.'

Mr Wilkinson, the Station master, a fussy little man, proud of the braid on his uniform, looked at his watch.

'I'm afraid I can only give you an extra five minutes. There's a coal train due through here in a quarter of an hour. They don't like trains arriving late at the collieries. Time lost means money wasted.'

Parents of the St Padarn's children on the platform were making rude comments about Bertie when he arrived, with the sweat trickling down his face. Tickets were distributed at lightning speed.

However, by now most of the window seats had been taken by the parish church children who jeered at the St Padarn's contingent as they fought their way into the compartments.

Charles, who was sporting a dilapidated college blazer, had been ordered by the Vicar to take charge of the parish church choirboys. As I passed his compartment his tortured face was framed in the window against a background of confusion created by a dozen young demons intent on tearing each other apart. I smiled at him but he never saw me. He must have been engaged in praying for deliverance.

I had decided to separate Tommy Harris and Percy to avoid any trouble over little Betty Evans. As it turned out I was saved the trouble. Idris and family were in one carriage, Betty Evans was in another with her parents. Tommy's parents were not present, probably because they could not afford to come. So I took him with me into a compartment full of children from the parish church Sunday School.

The train began to puff its way out of the station with Mr Wilkinson, the Station master, standing statuesque on the platform, the very embodiment of Great Western Railway officialdom.

The four seats by the window were occupied by militant young gentlemen who eyed Tommy with the scorn they felt due to a 'teacher's pet'.

'Can I pull the window down, sir, and look out?' asked Tommy.

'As long as you don't lean out of it. Otherwise you might get your head knocked off,' I said.

'I can knock his block off any time.' This *sotto voce* remark came from Sidney Jenkins, a corpulent ten-year-old who enjoyed throwing his weight around.

'Any more comments like that, Sidney,' I warned him, 'and I'll knock your block off.'

Tommy made his way to the window over the deliberately outstretched legs of the other boys. He pulled the window down and proceeded to rest his arms on the carriage door. Sidney's foot began to hook itself around Tommy's leg in harmony with the foot of Arthur Williams around the other leg.

Just as they were about to indulge in a joint exercise, I stood up.

'Sidney, Arthur, stand up!' I ordered. 'Come with me into the next compartment.'

A class of girls was in the next compartment under the control of Miss Myfanwy Evans, an elderly spinster who was feared throughout the parish church Sunday School.

'Have you room for two boys who have been misbehaving themselves, Miss Evans?' I asked.

It was a challenge she relished.

'Certainly. After yesterday's disgraceful proceedings, I should be only too pleased to take charge of them. Mair and Elspeth, you go with Mr Secombe.'

Tommy was still standing at the window when I returned and no one had dared to occupy the two vacant seats by the window. The two girls planted themselves in the corner and stared up at Tommy who now transferred his attention to the inside of the carriage.

'Would you like to look out, sir?' he asked, eyeing my seat by Elspeth.

'No, thank you, Tommy. You enjoy yourself.'

A few minutes later he came away from the window.

'I think I've got something in my eye, sir. I'd better sit down.' He was addressing Elspeth rather than me.

'Move over,' I said to the boy on the other side of me. 'Sit down, Tommy and let's see your eye.'

'It's all right, I think it's gone now.'

'Good. Anyway you can rest your eyes. We've a couple of tunnels coming up any minute now. You had better sit back and relax.'

Twenty minutes elapsed and we arrived at Llangelli Halt. A solitary porter was engulfed by the hordes who poured out of the train and into the station yard. 'Like Piccadilly Circus, innit?' he said to me.

'I've never been there,' I replied.

'Nor me, but they do say it is always crowded – a lot more than 'ere, anyway.' Then he pushed his way up to the front of the train to have a chat with the engine driver.

There was shrill blast on a whistle inside the station yard. It was Bertie.

'Now then, boys and girls. Get into your classes and we'll march down to the field.'

'What's the betting he leads us into the farmyard instead of the field,' said Idris.

'How far away is the field?' enquired the Vicar.

'About half a mile as the crow flies,' replied Bertie airily.

'We don't fly, Mr Owen. We shall have to walk. How far is it to walk?' The Vicar's temper was nearing the end of its short fuse.

'You can see the entrance to the farm from here, Vicar.' He pointed to a gate some distance along the main road. 'Then it's about three fields away from there on the right-hand side. No, wait a minute, on the left-hand side. Anyway, Vicar, follow me.'

The invitation was 'Dobson's choice', as Mrs Richards would say. We all followed Bertie as he proceeded down the main road carrying his suitcase and attempting unsuccessfully to whistle the song of the Seven Dwarfs from Walt Disney's cartoon.

'I suppose he knows the way,' said Father Whittaker to me. His anxiety was being shared by teachers and parents alike. The children were unaffected by such qualms. They were laughing, joking, jostling each other. Charles was a picture of abject misery as he tried to control the boisterous choirboys.

After twenty minutes' walk we reached the entrance to Gelli Farm, which announced its existence in red letters painted on a rough-hewn piece of wood. The smooth tarmac of the main road gave place to a pot-holed primitive road which sprouted large tufts of grass in two parallel lines. In the pot-holes, as the Psalter Book phrases it, were 'pools filled with water' which proved an irresistible attraction to the younger children. Immaculately clean white socks and canvas shoes were soon mottled with muddy water.

Ahead of the Pontywen Church column of marchers, the organiser strode on oblivious of the resentment building up behind him.

'Next year,' promised the Vicar, 'it's Barry Island and I shall organise the outing.'

Just as the discontent was about to explode there was a shrill blast on the whistle. Bertie stood and pointed like Moses surveying the Promised Land. At the far end of the field smoke was billowing from the parish boiler.

'Here we are, boys and girls!' he shouted. 'Now then get into line and you will each have a bag of sweets.'

He put down his suitcase and struggled to lift the heavy iron gate open. Two of Charles's protégés darted forward under the guise of helping but with the real intent of being first in the queue for the distribution of sweets. This sudden rush of assistance caught Bertie unawares. The gate shot backwards, depositing the Churchwarden and the two 'helpers' in two large fresh cowpats. The seat of Bertie's trousers was plastered in cow muck while the boys were more liberally anointed.

There was an outburst of laughter from the onlookers.

'That's enough of that,' shouted the Vicar. 'Wentworth-Baxter. I thought you were in charge of these boys.'

'They're not boys,' Charles expostulated, 'they're wild animals.' His limit of endurance had been strained beyond breaking point.

'Mr Owen, I think you had better go to the farmhouse with the boys and see what can be done about cleaning up. Leave your suitcase here and Mr Secombe and I will give out the sweets.'

Bertie and the two choirboys sped up the lane while the Vicar and I stood at the entrance, doling out the sweets.

When the last of the children had received their quota we made our way to the other end of the field where Reuben Hopkins was stoking up the boiler and the women were standing at the trestle tables, cutting bread and butter and seed cake.

'I hear Bertie Owen has put his foot in it once again,' Reuben said.

'It wasn't 'is foot,' replied Idris who had come to see if he could help. 'It was the other part where 'e keeps 'is brains.'

The Vicar pretended he had not heard the remark.

'When will the tea be ready?' he asked Reuben.

'About half-past three, Vicar. We generally have the races first. Bertie's got the money for prizes in his case. You've got to give the children and their parents time to settle down first of all.'

Settling down for the parents meant the spreading of mackintoshes on the grass and for the children exploring the terrain, which included a stream swollen by the rain of the past week.

'I think I had better go to the farmhouse to see what has happened to Mr Owen and the boys. I'll take his suitcase with me. Fred, you are in charge until I come back.' With these words, Father Whittaker made his escape from the field.

No sooner had he disappeared when Charles emerged from behind one of the bushes bordering the stream.

'Fred, I don't think I'll be able to last out the afternoon. These

167

kids are terrible. Before long one or more of them will fall in that stream. That will mean the high jump for me from our lord and master.'

With that, there was a yell from further down the stream. I turned around to see Percy clambering up the bank soaked to the skin, while Tommy Harris was running away from the scene as fast as his legs could carry him. Evidently he had decided to nobble his chief opponent in the races.

'Sorry, Charles, but it looks more like the high jump for me,' I said and ran down towards Percy.

'He pushed me in, sir, honest! I wasn't doing anything and he just came up behind me and shoved me in.'

'All right, Percy. I'll have words with Tommy Harris in a minute. In the meantime let's get to your parents and see about drying your clothes.'

Idris, Gwen and Elsie were about to enjoy a flask of tea and a sandwich when Percy and I arrived to put paid to their picnic.

'Percy!' exclaimed Gwen. 'You are getting a very naughty boy. Look at you. You'll catch your death of cold. Come here.'

'It's not his fault, Gwen,' I said. 'He was pushed into the stream by Tommy Harris. I'm going to deal with him now.'

That was easier said than done. Tommy had gone into temporary hiding. I was still looking for him when the Vicar arrived with Bertie Owen, whose lower limbs were encased in a pair of the farmer's trousers. Unfortunately for Bertie, Mr Pugh was some six inches shorter with the result that the bottom of the trousers ended where the Churchwarden's socks began.

Undeterred by his mishap, Bertie launched into his programme of races. While this was going on, Percy sat down with his father's raincoat around him and his clothes drying on the branches of a tree. Tommy Harris was nowhere to be seen.

Prompt at half-past three, tea was served in mugs which had Pontywen Church painted in bold letters. There was the inevitable competition to see who could drink the most mugs of tea. One boy claimed to have drunk six, a claim disputed by his neighbour who said he had seen him throw away three mugfuls when he thought no one was looking. By five o'clock preparations were being made to strike camp and make for the railway station. Percy's clothes had dried. The two choirboys had returned from the farmhouse, having enjoyed an enormous meal and boasting about it to the other boys.

During all this time there had been no sign of Tommy. 'We must organise a search party,' said the Vicar. Teachers and parents joined in the hunt for the missing boy. At half-past five the procession began back to the railway station where the train was due to leave at ten-past six.

I decided to go to the farm buildings to see if Tommy had hidden himself there. It was a wise decision. When I looked inside the barn I found him fast asleep on a bale of hay. I shook him by the shoulders. He stared at me for a moment.

'Are the races started yet, sir?' he asked.

'The races have come and gone. So has the tea. You've missed everything. That's what you get for pushing Percy in the stream. You'd better hurry now or you'll be missing the train as well.'

On the return journey Tommy was regarded with a certain amount of awe by the same boys who had scorned him previously. He was a public figure, a rebel and by no means a teacher's pet. He may have missed the races and the tea but he was enjoying his new-found kudos much more.

'Did you have a good day?' asked Mrs Richards later.

'Apart from the fact that we almost missed the train, that Bertie and two choirboys fell in cow muck, that Percy Shoemaker fell in a stream and that we lost a boy from our Sunday School, it was a great success.'

'Sounds a bit like that old Vicar's egg, six of one and a dozen of the other.'

'That about sums it up,' I said. 'Especially a dozen of the other. You ask Charles.'

16

'A fortnight to go, and this production is a shambles,' I moaned. 'Some of the principals still don't know their lines, while the Pirates are more like mice than men.'

'Nonsense!' said Eleanor. 'You have a delightful chorus of girls, far younger and prettier than any other operatic society's so-called maidens. The police are developing into a force to rival the Keystone Cops. Admittedly the Pirates are an anaemic body apart from Bertie Owen, who is so over the top that he could give a blood transfusion to the rest and still have a lot left for himself.'

'All right, that's the chorus but what about Trevor Willis? He comes to us, recommended by Idris as a seasoned performer in the Valleys. If his voice stays as croaky as it is, he is going to be an inaudible Major-General Stanley. Then there's Islwyn Jenkins who is as nervous as a kitten.'

'Well, my love, you can't say that his voice is croaky. You can hear that Pirate King's ringing tones two miles away. Once he's got his first performance over, he'll be excellent, believe me. Then there's Myfanwy Howells who makes a very good Ruth, Idris a very funny Sergeant of Police and, of course, the two leads who are absolutely brilliant.'

'Self praise is no recommendation but I must admit you are right.'

'I thought you would, you bighead. So cheer up, Frederick and let's go and see if they've started work on our little grey home in the west.'

We were seated in the front of her car after the Thursday rehearsal at Pontywen Grammar School.

'It's almost dark. We haven't a key. So how are we going to

know if anything is happening there?'

'My dear love, you are about as romantic as a wet lettuce. We'll be able to see something, even if it's nothing. Pardon the paradox, the most ingenious paradox.'

'Excuse me, Mabel,' I said, 'but that's one of my lines not yours.'

She replied by putting her foot on the accelerator and shooting off down the road. When we arrived outside our future home it was dark but a lamp-post opposite illuminated part of the front room.

'The furniture has gone. That's a start.' She squeezed my hand. 'So let's go to your digs and fix a date for our nuptials.' She planted a kiss on my cheek.

'You shameless hussy. What will the neighbours say? Not only that, when you talk about "nuptials" it sounds more like a Roman orgy than a wedding.'

'Come on, Clark Gable, let's consult the calendar. My mother is anxious to book a hotel for the reception and you'll have to book a church somewhere for the ceremonial.'

'I think I can manage that,' I said. She caught hold of my arm and steered me to the car.

A quarter of an hour later we were closeted in my room, consulting my *Parson's Pocket Book*, an essential for any conscientious curate. It contained a daily list of the lessons to be read throughout the year, a visiting list for each week and a calendar.

She flicked through the pages.

'According to this you have been visiting a large number of females in this parish. What have you to say for yourself, Secombe?'

'Guilty, my lord – I mean, my lordness, but before you pass sentence, I think you had better see these females for yourself.'

'Plea for mitigation accepted unreservedly without inspection of the said females. The sentence is a lenient one. You are ordered to allow me to choose the date myself.'

'I am entirely in your hands, your worship, your holy highness.'

'Very prudent. You see, if Frederick wishes to get Mabel in the end, then Mabel must decide the date.'

'Beautiful Mabel, I would if I could but I am not able,' I sang.

'Well, in that case, dear Frederick, it must be Saturday July 23rd. According to this diary, the eve of the Feast of St Mary Magdalene.'

'Most appropriate,' I said.

'What do you mean by that you wicked insinuator?' She put her hands on her hips and gave me a reproachful look.

'I mean by that, dear Eleanor, that Mary Magdalene was a most loving person.'

'Explanation accepted, with demonstration.' She put her arms around me and gave me a long lingering kiss.

'That's your lot for tonight,' she said. 'We'll carry on from there next time we meet.'

'Sunday evening seven-thirty p.m., Pontywen Grammar School Hall, if not before.'

'Certainly not before. I have much to do over these next weeks. So have you, if it comes to that. Unless we are going to do a Japanese squat, we must have chairs to sit on and a table to match – not to mention a bed to sleep on. I think we'd better have a long talk about this next Sunday evening.'

'Your every wish is my command, princess.'

'Sarcasm will get you nowhere, Secombe. See you Sunday.'

Since Mrs Richards had not yet retired for the night I thought I had better pass on the news that the wedding date had been fixed.

'Make a note of the twenty-third of July, Mrs Richards,' I said. 'Don't make any engagements for that day. It's *the* social event of the year in Pontywen.'

The old lady managed a smile.

'So that's when you and your young lady are getting sliced. It won't be long now. You'll be surprised how time flies past. I'm sure you will be very happy, like boys in the sand. Don't forget me when you go. Come and see me now and again.'

Her face had dropped and she was near to tears.

'I'll come and see you more than now and again. It will be quite often – just to keep an eye on you. I wonder if Charles would like to come here.'

'Mr Secombe, I don't think I could cope with that young man. I'm getting too old to look after a gibberty flibberty like him.'

Next morning when I called for Charles on my way to the daily service I told him that we had fixed a date for our wedding.

'Great!' he said. 'Do you think Mrs Richards will have me as a replacement? It's very awkward living over a fruit and veg. shop. Moelwyn and Myfanwy are very kind to me but it's not really the kind of place for a curate's residence.'

'Sorry, Charles,' I replied. 'I suggested that you might like to come in my place but she thinks she's too old to take on another lodger.'

His face dropped.

'However, my friend,' I went on, 'I should be more than delighted if you would take on the heavy responsibility of being my best man.'

'Fred, thank you.' He shook my hand. 'That is marvellous. I've never been a best man before. You must tell me what I have to do. I promise I'll do my best.'

By the time we reached the church he was so full of importance at the prospect of being my best man that he had forgotten his disappointment at having to remain at the greengrocer's shop.

When morning prayer was ended after the Vicar had smilingly addressed the Almighty at least half a dozen times in the prayers after the third collect, he invited us to the Vicarage for coffee.

Mrs Lilywhite entered the study with her usual batch of overfilled cups on the tin tray, a much used part of her kitchen equipment.

'Here we are, Father,' she said and dumped the tray on his desk. She was the only person in the parish who addressed the Vicar as 'Father'. Charles insisted that she must be of Irish ancestry and that her mode of address was the sole reason that he retained her as his housekeeper.

'I think the time has come that we must do more to encourage the young into our midst.' The Vicar leaned back in his chair. 'To that end, I am proposing to start a pack of cubs in the parish. I want you, Wentworth-Baxter, to take charge of them.'

Charles stared in disbelief.

'I have bought a training manual and I have been in touch with the Scout Commissioner for the area. He will arrange for you to see a neighbouring pack to give you some idea of what's involved.'

My colleague remained speechless. He was in a state of shock. In his mind he could see all those choirboys who had tormented him on Whit Monday as prospective wolves rather than cubs.

'Fred,' continued the Vicar, 'I know you are doing a great job with the young girls in your Gilbert and Sullivan Society but I'm concerned about the young lads of the parish. So I'm proposing that you start a boys' club.'

'Before you go any further, Vicar,' I interjected, 'I think you should know that Eleanor and I intend to get married on July 23rd. I was going to have a word with you today, in any case, about that. Under those circumstances don't you think it wiser to delay any plans for a club until the autumn. Perhaps the same could go for Charles as well.'

Charles looked at me as if I were a lifeboatman rescuing a drowning man.

Father Whittaker rose to his feet and offered me his hand. 'Congratulations, Fred. Are you getting married here or in Eleanor's parish?'

'Since Eleanor was brought up in Pontywen and now practises here, we should like to be married in the parish church.'

'Fine. Let's look at the marriage bookings.' He thumbed through a file of papers. 'There's a wedding booked for two o'clock. The rest of the day is free.'

'Shall we say twelve o'clock tentatively? I shall consult my bride-to-be and let you know definitely on Monday.'

'About the cub troop, Vicar, and the boys' club. Are we going to leave it till the autumn?' The plaintive tone of voice in Charles's question would have softened the hardest of hearts.

'It's a cub pack, Wentworth-Baxter. All things considered, with holidays et cetera ahead of us, it is probably just as well that we should start next September. However, it will not do any harm if you go to see what happens in cub scouting and read up the manual over the next few months.'

The condemned man heaved a sigh of relief at this temporary reprieve.

'Thanks, Fred, you saved my life.' He patted me on the back as we walked up the Vicarage drive.

'For the time being, that's all, Charles. It's just putting off the evil day.'

'Perhaps I can learn a few tricks from that Commissioner bloke.'

'Perhaps he will decide that you are not cub leader material and advise the Vicar to get a lay person. That's your best bet.'

174

'I never thought of that. I'll have to act dumb.'

'You don't have to act that, Charles, just be yourself.'

He gave me a quizzical look and left me for his digs.

Sunday's rehearsal was much more encouraging. The art master at the school had completed painting the flats for Act One and this had a psychological effect on the Company. The Cornish coastline was a much better background than the bare walls of St Padarn's. The 'Climbing over rocky mountains' chorus came alive against the setting. Even the pirates began to look as if they might have come from Penzance instead of Pontywen. Islwyn Jenkins began to relax more as the Pirate King but Trevor Willis sounded like a Major-General who spoke in whispers for fear of giving away military secrets.

Back in Mount Pleasant View, Eleanor professed herself well pleased with the evening's work but was more concerned about July 23rd.

'I've booked the church for twelve o'clock, if that's all right with you?' I said.

'Ideal. It means we can be eating by about half-past one. My mother has been in touch with the Monmouth Arms Hotel, and they have booked the date provisionally. She can confirm the booking now.'

'There's one important matter to discuss before we go any further.'

'Pray, tell Eleanor all about it.'

'I must buy you an engagement ring and, while I am about it, a wedding ring.'

'OK, Rothschild, when do you wish to indulge in these expensive purchases?'

'That's the whole point. They will not be expensive purchases.'

'Look, love, if you gave me a ring from a lucky dip I should be quite happy.'

'There's one other thing. I have not formally asked your father for your hand.'

'You quaint old-fashioned curate. It's a wee bit late to indulge in that courtesy. Don't forget that it was I who told my parents last year that I was going to grab your hand. In any case, my father would be as embarrassed as you would be.'

So we went to Cardiff the following Saturday and came back

175

with a pretty little diamond ring.

'You can save your coppers for the wedding ring till nearer the day,' she said when we arrived back at my digs. 'In the meanwhile isn't it time that you formally placed the ring on my finger and did a swalk?'

'Did a what?'

'Sealed with a loving kiss, you ignoramus.'

I performed both functions to our mutual satisfaction after which we went into the middle room to display the ring to Mrs Richards.

'I think it's a lovely ring. It suits you, dear, nice and not too ostenacious. I hope you'll both be very happy.'

The old lady gave Eleanor a hug and a kiss. Then she turned to me.

'You're a very lucky man to have a financée like this and so is she to have you as her future husband. You go together like a horse in a carriage.'

She caught hold of me and planted a large kiss on my cheek.

'Mrs Richards, this is so sudden,' I said.

The old lady blushed and then covered her embarrassment with an invitation to drink to our future happiness with the remainder of the bottle of brandy bequeathed her by her late husband.

The next week flew past and the Monday of the dress rehearsal arrived leaving me in mid air. In the morning I went down to Cardiff to buy make-up, plenty of sticks of two, five and nine grease paint, crepe hair, spirit gum, liners, tins of cream and powder. Eleanor and I had arranged to do the make-up between us, apart from Trevor Willis and Iorwerth Ellis who claimed to be masters of the art.

Mrs Collier, wife of the St Padarn's church organist, had volunteered to be Wardrobe Mistress. She had been a member of the Pontywen Amateur Dramatic Society and had acted in that capacity for them, either because of lack of histrionic talent or because she had been a dressmaker by trade. When I returned from Cardiff she was waiting for me at my digs.

'The costumes haven't come, Mr Secombe. They should have been here on the eleven forty-five from Newport. I've phoned the costume people and they said that they had put them on the train first thing this morning. Mr Wilkinson has phoned

Newport from our station but they haven't got them there.' She was on the verge of tears.

'Has he phoned Cardiff General Station? Perhaps they have gone there by mistake?'

'You know what he's like, Mr Secombe. It was quite an effort to get him to phone Newport.'

'Let's go round to Moelwyn Howells and get him to phone Cardiff.'

Since Moelwyn's wife had a leading part, he was only too pleased to help.

Mrs Collier and I waited with bated breath while he phoned Cardiff General Station. He held the phone in one hand and stroked his black moustache with the other.

'It's addressed to the Pontywen Church Gilbert and Sullivan Society.'

He shook his head and raised his eyebrows.

'The Pontywen Church Gilbert and Sullivan Society,' he repeated much more slowly.

He put his hand over the mouthpiece.

'They're either deaf or dull.'

'I don't care if they're both, as long as they find those skips,' I said.

It seemed an eternity before he shouted 'Good' and gave the thumbs up signal.

Then came the bad news.

'He says it won't be possible to get them here until tomorrow morning.'

'There's only one thing for it, Moelwyn, we'll have to go to Cardiff this afternoon and pick them up. You can't have a dress rehearsal without costumes.'

'How do you propose doing that, Mr Secombe? You can't go down on the bus and pick them up, that's positive.'

'Just tell them that somebody will be down at Cardiff General to pick them up.'

'They say that faith can move mountains,' commented Moelwyn. 'Perhaps it can move skips of costumes.'

As Mrs Collier and I were leaving the greengrocer's shop we met Mr Matthews the undertaker.

'Busy?' I asked him.

'Very quiet at the moment.'

'In that case could you do us a great favour? We are absolutely desperate and you are the one man who can help.'

'What kind of favour?'

I offered up what is known as an arrow prayer.

'There are two skips of costumes stranded at Cardiff Station and we must have them for our dress rehearsal tonight.'

'So?'

'Would it be possible for you or your driver to take the hearse down to Cardiff and pick them up. I would come with you and we'd pay the petrol.'

'A hearse is not licensed to carry goods, only bodies, Mr Secombe.'

'I thought you could pull down the blinds and then nobody could see inside. Mr Matthews, this is an emergency.'

The old man looked long at me.

'Be at my house in a quarter of an hour and not a word to anybody, you two.'

'Mr Secombe, you must have a lot of faith and persuasion to make Tommy Matthews do that. Well done.' Mrs Collier was most impressed.

Twenty minutes later a cleric and an undertaker were in the front of a hearse with drawn blinds speeding with unseemly haste to Cardiff Station, where two surprised porters found they were loading the skips into a very unlikely vehicle.

Back in Pontywen at the Grammar School where Mrs Collier was waiting, we transferred the skips into the school hall in time to escape the attention of any early bird in the cast.

'Forget the petrol money,' said the undertaker, 'but please never ask me to do that again. Will Book and Pencil would have had me for that.'

'I'm eternally grateful to you. You and Mrs Matthews will have complimentary tickets for the show.'

By the time the cast were arriving the costumes were unpacked and on coat hangers. Mrs Collier was a most systematic Wardrobe Mistress.

The girls were caught up in the excitement of trying on their Victorian costumes and their dressing room was a pandemonium of shrieks and giggles. I had asked the pirates to supply their own rugby jerseys and head scarves. They had also brought their own barrel of beer, unasked.

178

Eleanor rushed in after finishing her surgery, anxious to try on her dress before beginning her job as make-up artist. I was already wearing my costume as Frederick which had been accompanied by a hideous ginger wig, which I had no intention of wearing.

The next hour or so was a hectic time for the two of us plastering make-up on faces unaccustomed to such treatment. I had barely enough time to do my own make-up before the curtain was due to rise.

It was a typical dress rehearsal. Lines were fluffed. The orchestra, coming together for the first time, occasionally sounded as if they had not been introduced to each other. The Major-General's voice was still of the croaking variety but his stage presence was excellent. Islwyn Jenkin's Pirate King sang with an uncertain note and his stage presence was non existent. He looked as if he would rather be on his farm a thousand times, than on a Cornish beach in charge of a bunch of cut-throats. All the other principals were creditable and little Percy Shoemaker was quite a hit as a miniature policeman.

After the rehearsal was over, Aneurin the MD kept the orchestra back to iron out some of the difficulties encountered during the evening and then pronounced that he was 'reasonably satisfied'. Eleanor's verdict was equally favourable. 'For a company most of whom have never done anything before, they were very good.' Then she added, 'Tomorrow will prove that.'

Tomorrow came. The Vicar surprised Charles and myself by praying for God's blessing on the Pontywen Church Gilbert and Sullivan Society at Mattins. After service he told us that he was looking forward to the performance in the evening.

So, too, was Mrs Richards. 'I think it's wonderful what you have done with the Gilbert. It's brought a bit of life to Pontywen. You've been a real shot in the heart for us.'

Eleanor and I decided to ease the burden of make-up by letting some of the girls do their own now that they had seen what was involved. As far as the men were concerned, Trevor Willis offered to help since he did not have to appear until halfway through the first act and I had to be on stage for the opening.

Gwen Shoemaker was in charge of tickets and had managed to get an almost complete sell out. There was no shortage of volunteers for programme selling and ushering. All was set for an exciting first night.

At 6.30 p.m., an hour before curtain up, Will Book and Pencil appeared in the dressing room.

'I gather you're in charge, Mr Secombe. I've come to inspect the safety precautions. You must have all the emergency exits unlocked. I'll check those later. As far as fire regulations are concerned, have you got your wet blanket and a bath of water ready?'

'Sorry about that, Constable, but I'm afraid I haven't.'

'In that case, Mr Secombe, the show can't go on. I'll give you an hour to get the blanket. In the meanwhile I'll inspect your exits.'

Idris was standing near when the policeman delivered his ultimatum. As soon as Will had disappeared, he came to me with the offer of a blanket and a bath. 'I'll get Percy to go with me and we'll 'ave it 'ere in no time. Mind, it means we'll just be washing up and down as far as possible for the rest of the week.'

'Idris, you're a gem. I had thought of asking him to stay here for the week. He's the biggest wet blanket I've ever known.'

By the time the constable returned from his inspection Idris and Percy had returned with the blanket and the bath.

'I've inspected the emergency exits and they're all OK. Would you mind filling that bath with water before I go?'

Two of the chorus of policemen were deputed to take the bath to the tap and fill it. Dressed in their uniforms they placed it in front of him.

'Going to have a dip, Will?' asked Charlie Thomas.

'Never knew you was a Baptist,' added Harry Williams.

Will Book and Pencil glared at them.

'I'll tell you what. If there's going to be a fire behind here, you'll be glad I've arranged for the means to extinguish it. My job is to enforce the law and that's what I've done.'

'That's our job as well. As you can see, Will,' said Charlie, pointing to his uniform. 'We're in the same business as you, and what's more Idris there is a sergeant so I'd watch it if I was you, in case you go a bit too far in enforcing the law.'

PC Will Davies decided that the time had come to leave with whatever shreds of dignity he had left.

'All I can tell you is just watch it.'

Once he had gone, there were many outbreaks of laughter at his expense. His intervention had served to lighten the tension of first-night nerves.

At seven o'clock there was only one fly in the ointment and it was a big one. Islwyn Jenkins had not turned up. At the dress rehearsal he had been at the hall by half-past six. As the Pirate King he was due on stage shortly after the opening. Ten-past seven came and he was still an absentee. I was about to get somebody to phone his home from a call box when he arrived with his wife Rhiannon.

I was amazed to find him smiling and in an expansive mood.

'Hello, everybody,' he announced and quoted a tagline from a radio programme, 'I've arrived and to prove it I'm here.'

'Get dressed,' I ordered him, 'and Trevor will make you up.'

Rhiannon beckoned me and took me aside outside the dressing room.

'I'm sorry, Mr Secombe, but I'm afraid he's had too much to drink. He's been worried stiff about this part for weeks now. He'd arranged for somebody else to do the milking and he was in the house by half-past five. He was still upstairs at half-past six. So I shouted up to him, 'Islwyn, it's half-past six.' He came downstairs holding on to the banisters and looked at the barometer when he reached the bottom.

'"There you are," he said and pointed to the barometer, "It's early yet." So I knew he was tight. The smell of whisky was overpowering. I got him into the kitchen and gave him a big cup of black coffee. He's a bit better now and he'll sober up as time goes by. Islwyn is very good at holding his liquor. All I hope now is that he will sober up before he goes on.'

'Thank you, Rhiannon.' I put my arm round her shoulder. 'Don't worry, I'll get another cup of coffee to him straight away. You go out in the hall and enjoy it.'

'You're being funny, Mr Secombe. The one thing I'll enjoy is the final curtain and to know he's still standing on his feet.'

'It sounds more like a boxing match you're going to watch.'

'I suppose it's a bit like that. The survival of the fittest.'

With that she disappeared and I made my way to the kitchen and got Islwyn another cup of black coffee. Back in the dressing room he was being helped into his costume by a number of volunteers who could tell by the reek of spirits that Islwyn needed assistance of an urgent kind.

'Thanks boys!' he was booming out when I came in with a cup of black coffee. 'I'm going to slay 'em tonight, you wait.'

'Coffee for you, Islwyn. Drink this, it will lubricate your throat.' I put the cup in his hand. 'Nothing is better than coffee for your voice.'

'Is that right, Mr Secombe? Cheers everybody.' He raised the cup to his lips and downed the liquid as if he were parched with thirst.

There was a silent prayer from all in the dressing room. We sat him in a chair and Trevor Willis worked quickly on his face.

'I feel fine, Mr Secombe, marvellous,' boasted Islwyn.

'Keep quiet. Or I'll shove this stick of greasepaint down your throat,' Trevor threatened. It was effective.

For five minutes, there was nothing to be heard from the 'Pirate King'. Aneurin Williams, the musical director, entered the dressing room to see if everything was ready for the overture.

I took him outside and passed on the information about Islwyn.

'I'm afraid we might be in for some trouble.'

'What's that?' He looked alarmed.

'Islwyn is tight.'

'My God. What are we going to do?'

'He has had two cups of black coffee and his wife assures me that normally he can hold his liquor. I was once told of an MP who shall be nameless, recovering from an advanced state of inebriation to full command of his senses in half an hour. All we can do is to hope that Islwyn will do the same, but be prepared.'

'They're not all in their seats yet. So I'll hold fire for another five minutes or so.'

I went back into the dressing room. Trevor was powdering Islwyn's face. He finished by thrusting the puff inside his mouth, as he was about to speak.

'Put that in your cake hole and save your voice for the stage,' he commanded him.

'Would you like one more quick cup of coffee?' I asked.

'Yes, if it's good for the voice. I feel fine. I only hope my voice is all right.'

I disappeared into the kitchen and came back with the coffee to hear a very loud rendition of 'I am the Pirate King' coming from the other side of the closed door of the dressing room.

'One more cup of coffee and your voice will be in excellent form,' I assured him.

The coffee went down in one gulp.

'Ready for anything now,' he informed me.

There was a knock on the door.

I went out to find Aneurin looking apprehensive.

'Is he OK?'

'Well, he's on his feet. His voice could be heard miles away. So I assume he's ready for action.'

'I hope you're right. Good luck anyway.'

He shook my hand.

'The same to you, Aneurin, or better still. Shall we say it's in the Lord's hands.'

'Very much so,' he said and went out into the hall.

'Every pirate on stage,' I shouted and caught hold of Islwyn's arm.

'On form?' I asked.

'Raring to go.'

'What's your first line?'

'"Yes, Frederick, from today you rank as a full blown member of our band."'

'Well done,' I said and shook his hand.

'Not only that,' he went on, 'I'll act it as well.'

He did. His first words were accompanied with a heavy slap on my back which sent me reeling.

'Hurrah!' shouted the Pirates.

When eventually he reached his set piece solo, he was the embodiment of the Pirate King:

> And it is, it is a glorious thing.
> To be a Pirate King.

His rendition was greeted with rapturous applause. Islwyn Jenkins had arrived, with the aid of John Barleycorn, as a top class performer in Gilbert and Sullivan. However, just a few more drams and he would never have dared to appear again in amateur operettas.

Eleanor's singing of 'Poor Wandering One' received as much acclaim as Islwyn's solo. The first act was in full swing and all was well.

The scene was set for the entrance of the Major General. Samuel sings:

> We'd better pause or danger may befall.

The girls chorus:

> Their father is a Major-General.
> Yes, Yes he is a Major-General.

At this point in the proceedings, the Major-General suddenly appears on a rock, dominating the whole scene:

> Yes, Yes. I am a Major-General.

As he announced his arrival, in full military uniform bedecked with medals, and wearing his impressive plumed hat, the left half of his military moustache dropped off, to the intense amusement of the audience. To their even greater enjoyment, he searched on the floor, found his moustache, spat upon it and proceeded to sing the whole of the patter song 'I am the very model of a Modern Major-General' with his left hand pressing the recalcitrant piece of hair to his upper lip and his right hand gesticulating vigorously.

It was a forlorn effort and he spent the rest of the first act with the left upper lip bare and the right bristling with a moustache.

During the interval, the Vicar appeared in the dressing room to say how much he was enjoying the performance, while Charles confessed that he had never seen anything so funny in his life as the moustache incident. His appreciation of comedy was confined to slapstick. Eleanor thought that, considering the pre-performance alarms, it was amazingly satisfying.

In the second act, our love duet brought the place down, especially since we both had to declare our love for each other 'till we are wed and ever after'. The policemen's entrance was a riot with Idris at the head and Percy at the tail. A little later the Pirates entrance was equally as funny – unintentionally this

time because Bertie Owen was the only one out of step in the chorus 'With cat-like tread upon our prey we steal'. Islwyn's Pirate King was magnificent while the Major-General's moustache remained fixed throughout on the face of an accomplished character actor.

His appearance in a dressing gown, carrying a light, in his red slippers and night cap in the ruined chapel by moonlight, was a great success. His song 'Sighing softly to the river' was accompanied by a delightful piece of balletic dancing and his display of pathos at the Pirate King's pronouncement of a sentence of death for him was most convincing. Croaking voice or not, Trevor Willis was an acquisition for Pontywen Church Gilbert and Sullivan Society.

As we sang the Welsh National Anthem at the end of the performance, Eleanor and I stood side by side holding hands. When the curtain came down, we kissed each other.

'Now for stage two,' I whispered to her.

'Here endeth the first lesson, you mean,' she said. 'You've

learned an awful lot in your first year in Pontywen. You're certainly not as green as you were.'

'More like a man for all seasons.'

'More like a curate for all seasons, with a lot more to be learned.'